J.D. Salinger's
THE
CATCHER
IN THE
RYE

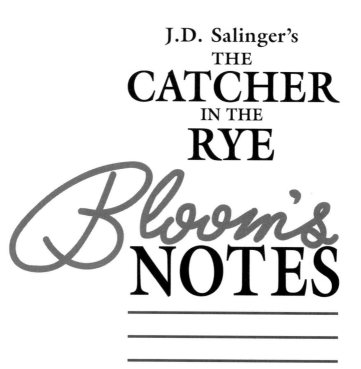

A CONTEMPORARY
LITERARY VIEWS BOOK

Edited and with an Introduction by
HAROLD BLOOM

Printed and bound in the United States of America.

First Printing
1 3 5 7 9 8 6 4 2

Cover illustration: Painting of Holden Caulfield by James Avati (1953) (photograph by Stanley Meltzoff).

Library of Congress Cataloging-in-Publication Data

The catcher in the rye / edited and with an introduction by Harold Bloom.
p.   cm. — (Bloom's Notes)
Includes bibliographical references (p.) and index.
ISBN 0-7910-3662-6
1. Salinger, J. D. (Jerome David), 1919– . Catcher in the rye. 2. Caulfield, Holden (Fictitious character) 3. Runaway teenagers in literature. 4. Teenage boys in literature. [1. Salinger, J. D. (Jerome David), 1919–. Catcher in the rye. 2. American literature—History and criticism.]
I. Bloom, Harold. II. Series: Bloom, Harold. Bloom's Notes.
PS3537.A426C329 1995
813'.54—dc20
95-23729
CIP

Chelsea House Publishers
1974 Sproul Road, Suite 400
P.O. Box 914
Broomall, PA 19008-0914

Contents

User's Guide

This volume is designed to present biographical, critical, and bibliographical information on J. D. Salinger and *The Catcher in the Rye.* Following Harold Bloom's introduction, there appears a detailed biography of the author, discussing the major events in his life and his important literary works. Then follows a thematic and structural analysis of the work, in which significant themes, patterns, and motifs are traced. An annotated list of characters supplies brief information on the chief characters in the work.

A selection of critical extracts, derived from previously published material by leading critics, then follows. The extracts consist of statements by the author on his work, early reviews of the work, and later evaluations down to the present day. The items are arranged chronologically by date of first publication. A bibliography of Salinger's writings (including a complete listing of all books he has written, cowritten, edited, and translated), a list of additional books and articles on him and on *The Catcher in the Rye,* and an index of themes and ideas conclude the volume.

Harold Bloom is Sterling Professor of the Humanities at Yale University and Henry W. and Albert A. Berg Professor of English at the New York University Graduate School. He is the author of twenty books and the editor of more than thirty anthologies of literature and literary criticism.

Professor Bloom's works include *Shelley's Mythmaking* (1959), *The Visionary Company* (1961), *Blake's Apocalypse* (1963), *Yeats* (1970), *A Map of Misreading* (1975), *Kabbalah and Criticism* (1975), and *Agon: Towards a Theory of Revisionism* (1982). *The Anxiety of Influence* (1973) sets forth Professor Bloom's provocative theory of the literary relationships between the great writers and their predecessors. His most recent books are *The American Religion* (1992) and *The Western Canon* (1994).

Professor Bloom earned his Ph.D. from Yale University in 1955 and has served on the Yale faculty since then. He is a 1985 MacArthur Foundation Award recipient and served as the Charles Eliot Norton Professor of Poetry at Harvard University in 1987–88. He is currently the editor of the Chelsea House series Major Literary Characters and Modern Critical Views, and other Chelsea House series in literary criticism.

Introduction

HAROLD BLOOM

The Catcher in the Rye is frequently compared to Mark Twain's *Adventures of Huckleberry Finn,* a dangerous comparison for Salinger's book, since Twain's work stands with Herman Melville's *Moby-Dick,* Walt Whitman's *Leaves of Grass,* Nathaniel Hawthorne's *The Scarlet Letter,* and Emily Dickinson's poetry as one of the handful of essential American books. Yet the link between Huck Finn and Holden Caulfield is palpable; Holden is necessarily one of the modern American descendants of Huck. For Huck there is still the frontier; he always can light out for the territory. Holden only has mid-century Manhattan, which will not provide him with the big river, Jim, and the raft. Alas, Manhattan gives Holden nothing positive; as many readers have noted, the city is his descent into Hell. Still, this may have more to do with Holden than with Manhattan. Like Huck, Holden is a boy of endless good will, but he is considerably less healthy than Huck, who is not a masochist. Holden is, and there is an element of doom-eagerness in his Manhattan adventures. Ambivalence, the simultaneous presence of positive and negative feelings in almost equal degree, dominates Holden throughout the book, in regard to his father, and to the entire adult world, but also to his own self.

We know Holden primarily as a narrative voice, which is the way we know Huck. Between Huck and Holden the clearest mediating figure is Nick Carraway, who narrates Scott Fitzgerald's *The Great Gatsby.* Carraway is a grownup who still shares in an adolescent's sensibility, and his admiration for Gatsby's greatness is echoed by Holden. Voice, properly modulated by a master storyteller, can tell us everything we need to know about a literary character, and there are few mysteries in Holden for the attentive reader. This is impressive because Salinger does not provide Holden with a very long foreground; what we learn, we learn directly by listening to Holden. He has lost his younger brother Allie to sickness and to death, and he is haunted by the loss; it is not too much to say that he is traumatized by it. Thirteen when Allie died, Holden is seventeen at the time of the novel, but his emotions remain arrested, as though he cannot grow older than he was then. Holden is a depressive who desperately needs help, but is too oppositional to seek it out. He suffers also from the guilt of a survivor, irrational guilt but immensely compelling.

And yet Holden, a vital and potentially strong consciousness, is considerably more than his illness, and is not to be regarded as a clinical study. He lacks the sturdiness of Huck Finn's spirit, and Huck's mythological largeness, but he has a spiritual eminence that is all his own. Distrusting all language, his own as much as any, he nevertheless has a faith in goodness and in love that invests him with authentic pathos. He will always remain vulnerable, but that is the cost of his confirmation as a kind of alienated saint, whose deepest wish is to be savior of children. Despite his sufferings, Holden remains an image of freedom, which is his most authentic inheritance from Huck Finn. Unlike Huck, who learns from Jim and from shrewdly observing everyone he encounters (except the tiresome Tom Sawyer), Holden scarcely is able to learn anything in the course of his book, because he cannot invest his trust in anyone who is not an image of innocence and he knows that only the dead and the very young are innocent. That makes survival very difficult for Holden, as he has no guides or teachers whom he can accept. And yet Holden does have a Huck-like genius for survival, despite his depressive doom-eagerness. At the end, lovingly watching his sister while the healing rain falls upon him, Holden becomes a figure of capable poignance, and persuades us implicitly that he will survive for some larger end or purpose, benign and generous in a more organized version of innocence. ❖

Biography of
J. D. Salinger

Jerome David Salinger was born on January 1, 1919, in New York City, the second child of Sol Salinger, a prosperous Jewish meat and cheese importer, and Miriam Jillich Salinger, a woman of Scottish-Irish descent. Salinger attended several public schools in New York before entering the McBurney School on the Upper West Side in 1932. He then enrolled at the Valley Forge Military Academy, where he edited *Cross Sabres*, graduating in 1936. In 1936–37 he studied at New York University, but left college to travel in Europe, where he wrote his first short stories. In 1938 he entered Ursinus College, writing a column for the school paper, but left after a semester.

In 1939 Salinger took a class in short-story writing at Columbia University, studying with Whit Burnett, founding editor of *Story* magazine. The next year he sold his first short story to *Story*, "The Young Folks" (published in the March–April 1940 issue). In 1942 Salinger was drafted in the U.S. army. After two years of training, he went overseas with the 4th Infantry Division, training with the Counter-Intelligence Corps in England and participating in the Normandy campaign and the liberation of France. He ultimately achieved the rank of staff sergeant, although his witnessing of some of the worst battles of World War II caused him to be hospitalized for a time with war-related stress. In 1945 he married a Frenchwoman named Sylvia (last name unknown), but divorced her the next year.

Returning to the United States, Salinger quickly began appearing widely in well-paying fiction magazines such as the *Saturday Evening Post, Collier's,* and the *New Yorker*. Between 1941 and 1954 he contributed some twenty stories to the "slicks," but in later years he repudiated much of this work. When a two-volume pirated edition of his *Complete Uncollected Stories* appeared (sometime between 1967 and 1974), he took legal action to have the edition suppressed.

The work Salinger wishes to be remembered for begins with the publication of "A Perfect Day for Bananafish" (*New Yorker,*

31 January 1948), about the suicide of Seymour Glass. This story is the touchstone for all the stories about the Glass family: those in *Nine Stories* (1953); *Franny and Zooey* (1961; consisting of two stories, "Franny" [*New Yorker*, 29 January 1955] and "Zooey" [*New Yorker*, 4 May 1955]); *Raise High the Roof Beam, Carpenters and Seymour—An Introduction* (1963; consisting of "Raise High the Roof Beam, Carpenters" [*New Yorker*, 19 November 1955] and "Seymour" [*New Yorker*, 6 June 1959]); and others. The Glass family stories concern the efforts of flawed, well-meaning people to deal with the essential hypocrisy of the world, and they are told from the viewpoints of various members of the Glass family. They range in tone from the kindness of Esmé in dealing with a psychologically shattered soldier in "For Esmé—with Love and Squalor" to the dark hopelessness of "Pretty Mouth and Green My Eyes."

Salinger's most famous work is *The Catcher in the Rye* (1951), one of the most popular novels of the latter half of the twentieth century. It tells the story of Holden Caulfield's struggle against hopelessness in a hypocritical world following his expulsion from prep school (which is probably modeled upon Salinger's own years at the Valley Forge Military Academy). Much of the book is cynical in tone, but Caulfield's despair is tempered with love for his sister and a vague sense of purpose in life. The book struck a powerful chord with the disenchanted yet idealistic youth of the Fifties and with an adult audience also conscious of repression and conformity. It has become a classic story of adolescence and continues to be read widely.

For a time in the Fifties many considered Salinger the most accomplished writer of fiction in America. His reputation has declined somewhat since the mid-Sixties, perhaps because he has published no new fiction since "Hapworth 16, 1924" (*New Yorker*, 19 June 1965). In the winter of 1952–53 Salinger purchased a country house in the remote village of Cornish, New Hampshire. He married Claire Douglas in 1955; they had two children, Margaret Ann and Matthew, before divorcing in 1967. Since that time Salinger has lived as a virtual hermit, although there are reports that he is continuing to write. In 1987 he appeared in court to prevent the publication of Ian Hamilton's biography of him, claiming that Hamilton's quotation and paraphrasing of his unpublished letters constituted copyright infringement. Salinger won the suit, and Hamilton's biography appeared the next year in a severely rewritten form. ❖

Thematic and Structural Analysis

In the first paragraph of *The Catcher in the Rye* J. D. Salinger sets forth one of the novel's major themes, that the self may be constructed in narrative. Holden Caulfield begins his story in the style of a psychoanalytic project that he will tell on his own terms. He engages the reader directly, but the narrative is suspect and unreliable by the awkwardness of its adolescent diction, by abrupt shifts in narrative stance, and by the mental instability revealed in the experiences, what he calls the "madman stuff," that have led to his physical and nervous breakdown. The second theme of the novel is the struggle toward adulthood through adolescence. The troubled seventeen-year-old narrator frames a chaotic rite of passage into adulthood within an account of the events of two days.

The Catcher in the Rye is a modernist novel because it focuses upon the narrator's inner perceptions, solipsism, and alienation from the community. As a post–World War II novel, it may be considered post modernist because it is also about writing. That is, it imagines the self as a fiction composed in and by narrative. Holden's first-person narrative is fragmented, juxtaposing observations of events and people with digressive explanations of his state of mind. That he does so within the confines of a sanitarium suggests that his narrative has a therapeutic purpose. It may restore him to the social world. Although he will not discuss the "David Copperfield kind of crap" of his childhood, by his frequent references to novels, to classics he has particularly liked, we know that they have given him clues to human character but, as yet, little insight into himself.

Holden's brother D. B. is a Hollywood screenwriter whom he both admires as a success and disparages as a literary prostitute. He hates movies for their "phoniness" but will refer to them frequently. Of D. B.'s work, Holden most admires a short story written while he was still a "regular writer," before he went to Hollywood. "The Secret Goldfish" is about a child who has purchased a goldfish and will not let anyone see it. He offers no analysis. But, imagistically, nothing is less private than a goldfish in a bowl, or less interesting. It suggests itself as a model of Holden's lonely resistance to adulthood. Holden lives an insulated life within inescapable social and economic parameters. He suspects, perhaps rightly, that his problems are of little interest to anyone. His sanity resides in the construction of a coherent narrative. He may have subtext, but he must first have a story.

"Where I want to start telling is the day I left Pencey Prep," he tells us. The **first seven chapters** focus upon Holden's experience at a prestigious Pennsylvania boarding school. He begins the story of his emotional and physical deterioration on the cold December day of the last football game of the season. Holden stands at the top of a hill, next to a Civil War cannon, observing the game as if it were a battle. He muses on the absence of girls and recalls the headmaster's daughter as a plain but "nice girl" who probably knew that her father was a "phony." The girl's opinion is never confirmed. He stands on the hill because he was the captain of the fencing team and had lost the equipment en route to a game. The other reason is that he is on his way to say good-by to his history teacher. "I forgot to tell you about that. They kicked me out," he continues, for academic failure, a situation that, we later learn, has occurred repeatedly. Holden waits to "feel some kind of a good-by," some incident or memory by which he may know he is leaving Pencey. He recalls an evening chucking a football around with two friends. This is enough. "I was lucky," he says about the superstitious ritual of memory that releases him. Holden's ritual does not signify emotional growth. It works as a device by which he may move, not toward adulthood, but only away from one episode into another. A similar suggestion of psychological frailty is embedded in the sensation he describes as a feeling of disappearing "every time you crossed a road." This theme of invisibility, of disappearing, is most prominent in Holden's moments of greatest despair, and he will describe it most vividly in chapter twenty-five. In **chapter one** this irrational fear compels him toward the next contact, Mr. Spencer, the history teacher, and his wife. Holden betrays his class consciousness when he recalls that they had no maid and "always opened the door themselves." The slightly deaf wife sends him into Mr. Spencer's room. The elderly couple is a variation upon another teacher and wife, the Antolinis, whom Holden will visit in chapter twenty-three.

"People never notice anything," Holden concludes at one point in **chapter two.** He is six-foot-two-and-a-half-inches tall and has some prematurely gray hair, but he often acts, in his father's opinion as well as his own, as if he were twelve instead of seventeen years old. But not always, he complains. When he enters Mr. Spencer's bedroom he observes as many details as possible: the Vicks Nose Drops, the smell of medicine, an old bathrobe, nose picking, the phony word "grand" his teacher uses to describe Holden's parents, the *Atlantic Monthly,* the bed "like a rock," the elderly man's chest beneath his bathrobe. He can describe appearances but cannot read into character or intent. Mrs. Spencer liked him. "At least," he recalls, "I think she did."

In **chapters three through five** Holden narrates a cluster of incidents and impressions that point to the theme of the narrated self. He declares himself "the most terrific liar you ever saw in your life" in chapter three. We already realize that the detailed impressions he foregrounds have not affected him more than being expelled from school or leaving the fencing equipment on the subway, as he would have us believe. He counters his confession of deceit with an example of more pernicious lying in the story of "Old Ossenburger," a school benefactor who runs a national chain of funeral parlors and claims to talk to God. Presumably, Holden thinks, he asks Him for "more stiffs." Ossenburger's story of success and useful religion is a parodic overview of the adult capitalist world that alienates him. But Ossenburger is a bore by anyone's standards and his speech is met with a resounding fart from the ranks of students in this captive audience. The famous red hunting hat is introduced in *chapter three,* purchased for a buck after the fencing equipment debacle.

"I'm quite illiterate, but I read a lot," he dryly offers, after taking off his coat and putting on the red hunting hat. He pulls the peak of the cap around to the back of his head and sits down to read Isak Dinesen's *Out of Africa,* a book he has gotten "by mistake" but likes very much. He admires the writing of D. B.,

Ring Lardner, Somerset Maugham, and Thomas Hardy, as well. Except for Maugham, for reasons he does not tell, Holden would like each as a "terrific friend." He is interrupted by a boy from the adjoining dorm room, Robert Ackley, who comes through the shower that separates the rooms. His emergence from the shower curtains comically deconstructs baptismal metaphors of transformation and rebirth, as well as any notions of cleanliness. Ackley proves that neither literacy nor personal hygiene has anything to do with privilege. He pushes the book back to see the title and Holden gives up trying to read. "You couldn't read anything with a guy like Ackley around. It was impossible." Ackley is a visible slob. Stradlater, Holden's self-centered and attractive roommate, is a "secret slob," well-groomed with a rusty razor.

In **chapter four** Stradlater asks Holden to write a composition for him on "anything descriptive" for an English class. Holden has been expelled for failing every subject except English, and he notes the irony of his position as he considers Stradlater's request. Stradlater puts on Holden's Vitalis and jacket and prepares to meet what turns out to be an old friend of Holden's, Jane Gallagher. Suggestions of sexual impropriety by her drunken playwright-stepfather, her nonsensical hoarding of kings in games of checkers, her mother doing "about a hundred and seventy" for nine holes of golf, and the familiar details of his innocent friendship with the girl contrast the sexual intentions Holden suspects Stradlater has toward her—in Holden's clothes. He pulls the peak of the cap around to the front, "for a change," and thinks about Jane. "It made me so nervous I nearly went crazy." Ackley comes through the shower curtains again, mercifully changing the subject. Holden and Ackley join another student for a trip to a movie and Holden vividly recalls an incident that seems, at first, related to nothing.

While his companions prepare for the trip to town, in the **fifth chapter,** Holden opens the window and makes a snowball in his hands. He starts to throw it at a car, then at a hydrant, but changes his mind because they are "too nice and white." He closes the window and keeps the snowball in his hand until the bus driver makes him throw it out, even though he had told the man he "wasn't going to chuck it at anybody." "People never believe you," he observes. Holden had no conscious idea, then or at the time of his narrative, of what he would have done with that snowball.

The boys do not see the movie and return to the dorm early, whereupon Ackley begins another repulsive grooming ritual and an often repeated description of a sexual encounter the previous summer. "He was a virgin if I ever saw one," Holden remarks. The boys finally leave and Holden puts on pajamas, bathrobe, and hunting hat and writes a story about his dead brother Allie's baseball mitt. By its juxtaposition with the episode of the snowball, the baseball mitt seems linked with the snowball that Holden could not throw and could not drop. But the association is unconscious, intuitive. Salinger allows no authorial intrusion to explain or to distract us from Holden's adolescent limits and confusion.

Allie, two years younger than Holden and "about fifty times as intelligent," died of leukemia at age thirteen. His baseball mitt is covered with poems he had written in order to "have something to read when he was in the field and nobody was up at bat." Holden "happens to have" the mitt in his suitcase and copies the poems, changing his brother's name so that it appears to be about Stradlater's brother. Like Stradlater wearing Holden's clothes and using his Vitalis, he may also use his talent and his brother. But Holden seems somehow aware of the irony of such appropriation. Although he loses nothing in the transactions (things are returned and the memory of his brother is still his own), they confirm his loneliness and alienation. When Allie died, Holden broke all the windows in the garage with his fist. His parents wanted him psychoanalyzed. "I don't blame them. I really don't," he tells us.

"Some things are hard to remember," Holden tells us at the opening of **chapter six.** Stradlater returns from his date with Jane, reads the composition, rejects it, and comments with cruel accuracy, "No wonder you're flunking the hell out of here. . . . You don't do one damn thing the way you're supposed to." Holden is more interested in finding out what happened on the date with Jane. Angry that his roommate may have compromised the innocence of his friend, Holden baits him into a fight and loses. Afterward, he puts on his red hunting hat, peak to the back, and admires his bloodied face in the mirror. "All that blood and all sort of made me look tough," he remarks.

In **chapter seven** Holden leaves Pencey Prep—before the Christmas break and before his parents have received notification of his expulsion. **Chapters eight through twenty** chronicle his twenty-four-hour odyssey homeward. He pulls the ear flaps of the hunting hat down and walks to the train station, washes the blood from his face with snow, and boards a train for New York. He tells us that he usually likes to read romance stories in magazines, but not this time. He removes his hunting hat and puts it in his pocket. An attractive woman, about forty, boards the train and sits next to him. She leaves her bags in the aisle and Holden considers how very irrationally he likes women, simply because of the way they might leave bags in the middle of an aisle. Coincidentally, she is the mother of a classmate at Pencey. He introduces himself by the name of the dorm janitor. On the assumption that "all mothers are slightly insane" he lies, telling her that her son, known for "snapping his towel at people's asses," is the most popular boy at Pencey. He offers her a cigarette. She notices that his nose is bleeding. He offers to buy her a cocktail. She observes that the club car is closed. He tells her he is going home early because he has a brain tumor, then turns his attention to a timetable "just to stop lying." He is either a born novelist or a born liar. We are not told what the woman thinks.

Arriving at Penn Station in **chapter nine**, Holden enters a phone booth to call "somebody." D. B. is in Hollywood; his sister, Phoebe, would be asleep and his parents might answer; and Jane is still at school. His old girlfriend, Sally Hayes, sent him a "phony letter" inviting him to trim her Christmas tree, but her mother thinks he is "wild" and "has no direction in life." This is one of the few indications Salinger gives the reader of how Holden is perceived socially. He takes a cab uptown toward his parents' apartment until he remembers his plan to stay in a hotel until vacation formally begins. He asks an incredulous cab driver where the ducks on the Central Park lagoon go in the winter, a query he will make of every cab driver he encounters. He puts his red hat on in the cab, but removes it before entering the hotel in case they would think him a "screwball." His room faces the windows on the other section of the hotel where he observes the behavior of "perverts and morons," notably a transvestite and a couple who spit water at each other. He tries to think rationally about his own sexuality but only concludes, disgustedly, that "In my mind, I'm probably the biggest sex maniac you ever saw." Holden juxtaposes his sexual frustration with a loving description of his sister, Phoebe, in **chapter ten.** The innocence and clarity of childhood love reassures him.

Not yet tired, Holden decides to go downstairs to the hotel nightclub. He thinks of calling ten-year-old Phoebe, because he wants to talk to "somebody with sense." He decides against it because he might have to hang up on his mother. Like many mothers, in the beliefs of their children, she is "psychic" and would know who it was. Unlike Holden, Phoebe is an achiever. "I'm the only dumb one," he tells us twice as he describes her and compares himself to his brothers. In this episode Holden alludes to the closeness he had with his younger brother, Allie. Like his feelings about being thrown out of Pencey or causing the fencing team to forfeit, he avoids telling what he suffers most. The sense is that Holden's childhood ended with the death of his brother, which is objectively true in two ways. The bond of his closest childhood relationship was severed by death, and his simultaneous arrival at adolescence required then, as it still does, that he continue no longer as a child.

In the hotel bar Holden offers to buy drinks for three thirty-ish female tourists. His observations of the three women are casually cruel and class-conscious. As they scan the room in vain for movie stars, Holden notes that they drink Tom Collinses "in the middle of December, for God's sake. They didn't know any better." But one woman is a very good dancer and Holden is "half in love" by the time they sit down again. Whenever any girl does "something pretty," Holden is momentarily, helplessly, in love.

The bar closes and, on his way back to his room, Holden recalls the afternoon with Jane Gallagher when they "came close to necking." He more fully explains the questionable behavior of Jane's stepfather that he alluded to in chapter four. He suspects that the man has made some sexual advance toward her, but Jane denies it. Between Holden and Jane there is an innocent affection that contrasts the vulgarity he perceives in adult sexuality. The hotel depresses him and he takes a cab downtown to Ernie's, a nightclub he has visited with D. B. Holden is both intrigued and repulsed by the sense that Ernie, a pianist, sounds when he plays like someone who would only talk to a "big shot." Ironically, Holden is of the class of American capitalists from which such big shots emerge. His ambivalence toward the music and the clubs reflects his ambivalence toward his social birthright.

New York City shapes much of Holden's story. The urban landscape contains him and the cold December night seems to confirm his isolation. His memories of love, family, and belonging are of summer, and they are correspondingly warm. Upon the urban grid he may locate family, money, class distinctions, community, entertainment, and his future. The only frontier for the dissatisfied, adolescent narrator is the condition of adulthood that looms at the edge of his own sanity.

Salinger's novel is implicitly critical of American capitalism or, at least, American capitalists. Holden and all his friends attend prestigious boarding schools and may aspire to the Ivy League. His father wants him to go to Yale or Princeton, but Holden says he would not, even if he were "dying." In fact, he may very well die if he is unable to conform to his father's wishes or more clearly define his own. He has already thought of suicide and his health has declined with his mental state.

Holden's appointment with a young prostitute, in **chapter thirteen,** is both moving and hilarious. He thinks it might be good practice, in case he ever marries. He falls over his suitcase on the way to open the door for the girl and notices that, when offered a cigarette, she fails to say thank you. "She just didn't know any better," he says. Hoping to appear confident, he introduces himself as "Jim Steele," but he soon decides he would rather just talk. He tells her that he is recovering from a serious operation. "I was a little premature in my calculations," he explains. The episode concludes violently in **chapter fourteen,** when he is badly beaten by Maurice, the elevator man and pimp, for more money. Imitating a film, he pretends that Maurice has shot him. He imagines himself staggering downstairs, shooting Maurice, crawling back to his room, and calling Jane. "The goddam movies," he says. "They can ruin you." Still not tired, Holden considers suicide, but the idea of becoming a spectacle changes his mind.

In **chapter fifteen** Holden encounters two nuns at Grand Central Station. He insists that they accept a charitable contribution. They are schoolteachers and ask what Holden has read. "She certainly didn't sound much like a nun," he thinks, in her enthusiasm for *Romeo and Juliet*. He tells them that Mercutio's death upset him because, unlike the title characters whose deaths were their own fault, his had been someone else's fault. "What school do you go to?" one nun asks. We cannot know what they think, but the nuns are predictably kind. Woven into the theme of isolation and alienation, religious bigotry mirrors the exclusiveness of social class. "Catholics are always trying to find out if you're a Catholic. . . . I'm not saying I blame Catholics," he concludes, unwittingly blaming Catholics. In **chapter seventeen** he lists Catholics among boys' boarding school cliques, all after the same goal—to be smart enough to buy a Cadillac.

Holden walks toward Broadway to look for a record, "Little Shirley Beans," as a gift for Phoebe. A "sort of poor" family is walking on the sidewalk and he hears the small boy singing, "If a body catch a body coming through the rye." It makes him feel "not so depressed," but he does not yet explain. He walks toward the Museum of Natural History, where Phoebe's friend said she might be, and describes what is best about the museum. No matter how the viewer had changed, in the exhibits "Nobody'd move." Unlikely to meet anyone he knows, Holden puts on the hunting hat. "Certain things they should stay the way they are," he concludes.

In **chapter twenty** Holden is drunk, exhausted, and moving rapidly toward mental and physical collapse. His adolescence has become a physical and psychological gauntlet. Loss of all kinds, confusions of truth and lie, irony and absurdity, have left him exhausted and near despair. On his way to the lagoon in Central Park to determine, once and for all, the whereabouts of those ducks, "something terrible happened." He drops and breaks the record he had bought for Phoebe. Looking for the ducks, he nearly falls into the pond, then sits on a bench, shivering, with ice in his hair. He wonders how Phoebe would feel if he died of pneumonia and recalls visiting Allie's grave where "It rained on the grass on his stomach." He walks home.

His parents are not at home and Holden talks with Phoebe in **chapters twenty-one through twenty-three.** His depression and despair upset his sister and she realizes he has been expelled from school. She challenges him to name one thing he likes. He can think only of the nuns and the boy from a former prep school who, harassed by a group of boys, hurled himself from a window and died. He tells Phoebe that he likes Allie, and that he likes sitting with her, talking. Frustrated with his answers, she asks him to name something he would like to be. He tells her he would like to be "the catcher in the rye," whose job it would be to catch children before they could fall over the cliff, out of innocence. "Daddy's going to kill you," Phoebe remarks. He tries to explain why he hates Pencey, but Phoebe cannot understand him. She hides her face in the pillow. He realizes that he has left childhood behind, in spite of himself. Phoebe gives him most of the money she has saved to buy Christmas gifts. Overwhelmed by his sister's unconditional love, Holden cries. A child offering comfort to another child, she tells him that he can sleep with her. He gives her his red hunting hat and leaves the apartment.

Still unable to face his parents, Holden calls his old English teacher Mr. Antolini, who invites him to stay there. Mr. Antolini is urbane, sophisticated, and witty in a way that reminds Holden of D. B. Holden describes his academic difficulties at Pencey and gives a harrowing description of a class called Oral Expression. Mrs. Antolini, much older than her husband, serves coffee and goes to bed. Mr. Antolini eventually follows her and Holden falls asleep on the couch. "Then something happened, I don't even like to talk about it." Mr. Antolini makes sexual advances and Holden, frightened and upset, leaves the apartment, telling the man that he has to pick up his bags at the station.

Holden takes a subway to Grand Central Terminal in **chapter twenty-five,** retrieves his bags, and sleeps for a couple of hours on a bench. He wonders if he has been unfair to Mr. Antolini, remembering his kindness in allowing him to come over so late and in advising him. He recalls that Mr. Antolini was the only one who would touch the dead boy who had committed suicide at school. He had wrapped the boy in his coat. The boy had been wearing Holden's sweater.

As Holden walks up Fifth Avenue toward home, "something very spooky" happens. Almost delirious, sweating in the cold air, and increasingly ill, he imagines that, when he steps off a curb, he may disappear before he reaches the other side. Ritualistically, he asks Allie to keep him from disappearing. Exhausted, he finally rests on a bench and decides to run away. He could pretend he is a deaf mute, he thinks, and never have to endure "useless conversations" again. He leaves a message for Phoebe at her school telling her to meet him at the Metropolitan Museum of Art so he may return her "Christmas dough" and say good-bye. She arrives, wearing Holden's hunting hat and dragging a suitcase, intending to accompany him. He tries to take her back to school. Angrily, she refuses to go and they walk, arriving at last at the carousel in the park. It starts to rain and Phoebe takes the hunting hat off and puts it on her brother's head. Again he cries as he is overwhelmed by love for his sister, his family, and by shared human frailty.

"That's all I'm going to tell about," Holden declares in the **final chapter.** He regrets having told as many people as he has about the two days after he left Pencey. We may read *The Catcher in the Rye* as a story about two days that led to a seventeen-year-old boy's nervous breakdown. More productively, we may read it as a novel about constructing a coherent narrative out of chaotic experience; about constructing meaning. Holden feels he is "missing" everyone he told about— Stradlater, Ackley, and even "that goddam Maurice." They have become characters in an idiosyncratic narrative that may be read, reread, and misread. To compose a story of one's self, as Holden Caulfield does, one engages in a psychoanalytic project. But, Salinger suggests, the process of making meaning engenders fiction and loss. ❖

—*Tenley Williams*
New York University

List of Characters

Holden Caulfield is the seventeen-year-old protagonist and narrator of *The Catcher in the Rye*. A prep school student coming of age in the late 1940s, he has become an emblem of the alienated youth portrayed in American literature and films since World War II. His insulated life of privilege is ironically undercut by the misery of life at a boys' boarding school. As a son of wealthy parents, he grew up in New York City and lived at home until sent to a series of boarding schools from which he has been dismissed for academic failure. The expectations of class and gender are that he will eventually attend an Ivy League college, but Holden has faltered on the "phoniness" that he finds impossible to ignore in the social fabric that envelops him. Briefly, when he asks Sally Hayes to run away with him, Holden seems to consider an alternative to the life prescribed for him, but the girl and the escape are impossible and he turns his confusion and anger inward upon himself. Caught in a paradox of adolescence, Holden looks inward, but he cannot bear to know what is there.

After a nervous breakdown confines him to a sanitarium, Holden tries to make some sense of the events leading to his condition. He is consumed by feelings of alienation from all community, including his family. He details impressions and descriptions of various people and events, but he reveals his most painful thoughts as if by accident. He reveals only by implication his distress at failing his parents, losing the fencing equipment, failing to protect Jane from Stradlater, his anguish over the loss of his younger brother, and his changing relationship with his younger sister, Phoebe, as he moves out of innocence. At the same time, his sexual inexperience is increasingly troublesome. Holden is an idealist and a romantic who genuinely likes women. He would like to resolve this with his conviction that he is, secretly, "the biggest sex maniac you ever saw."

In the turmoil of his adolescent thinking, opinions and ideals contradict each other, and he has only begun to find strength in a healthy sense of irony. His central dilemma is that he wants to retain a child's innocence, solipsism, and clarity, but because of biology he must move into either adulthood or madness. As a sort of compromise, he imagines himself "the catcher in the rye," a protector of childhood innocence exempt from movement into adulthood, which is neither possible nor sane.

Phoebe Caulfield is Holden's ten-year-old sister. The innocence and purity of his love for her is the childhood ideal Holden fears losing. He confides his misery over school and his expulsion, but she cannot understand him anymore. Her physical expressions of affection, although still innocent, seem inappropriate to him now that he has entered into adolescence. "Roller skate skinny," Phoebe is a decidedly sane and productive child who loves and admires her brothers, and busily composes experimental narratives about a girl detective, perhaps narrating something of herself in the process.

D. B. Caulfield is Holden's older brother. A writer, screenwriter, and World War II veteran, he visits Holden in the sanitarium and wants him to talk about his breakdown more than Holden would like.

Allie Caulfield is Holden's younger brother, dead of leukemia at age thirteen. He was a "wizard," loved by teachers and adored by the family. Although he has been dead two years, Holden has not recovered from the loss of this brother and close friend.

Mr. Antolini is Holden's former teacher from one of the many prep schools he has attended. Although Holden is shocked and frightened by his sexual advances, he considers that he has a generous and humane spirit. He remembers Mr. Antolini wrapping the young suicide victim in his own coat and begins to realize the complexities of people other than himself. ❖

Critical Views

[Harvey Breit (1909–1968), a longtime columnist and editor at the *New York Times Book Review*, wrote *The Writer Observed* (1956) and coedited Malcolm Lowry's *Selected Letters* (1965). In this review of *The Catcher in the Rye*, Breit is among the first to point out both the parallels and the differences between Holden Caulfield and Huck Finn.]

Somewhere about halfway in Salinger's novel, the bright, terrible, and possibly normal sixteen-year-old protagonist follows a little boy who is singing quietly to himself "If a body catch a body coming through the rye." Later when the youthful hero's younger sister challenges him, demanding to know if there is anything in the world that he likes or wants to be, he can only think he wants to be "the catcher in the rye." It is significant because the novel, for all its surface guilelessness, is a critique of the contemporary, grown-up world.

It isn't important whether Salinger had it in mind or not, but reading *The Catcher in the Rye* made me think of *Adventures of Huckleberry Finn*. Holden Caulfield struck me as an urban, a transplanted Huck Finn. He has a colloquialism as marked as Huck's: "You remember I said before that Ackley was a slob in his personal habits? Well, so was Stradlater, but in a different way. Stradlater was more of a secret slob. He always looked all right, Stradlater, but for instance, you should've seen the razor he shaved himself with. It was always rusty as hell and full of lather and hair and crap." Like Huck, Holden is neither comical nor misanthropic. He is an observer. Unlike Huck, he makes judgments by the dozen, but these are not to be taken seriously; they are conceits. There is a drollery, too, that is common to both, and a quality of seeing that creates farce.

What is crucial is where Huck and Holden part company. T. S. Eliot once pointed out that we see the world through Huck's eyes. Well, we do not see it through Holden's. We see Holden as a smiling adult sees a boy, and we smile at his spectral, incredible world. I think that is the decisive failure: whatever is serious and implicit in the novel is overwhelmed by the more powerful comic element. What remains is a brilliant *tour de force,* one that has sufficient power and cleverness to make the reader chuckle and—rare indeed—even laugh aloud.

—Harvey Breit, "Reader's Choice," *Atlantic Monthly* 188, No. 2 (August 1951): 82

S. N. BEHRMAN ON HOLDEN'S INNOCENCE

[S. N. Behrman (1893–1973) was a well-known dramatist as well as a critic and book reviewer. In this review, Behrman notes how the innocence and naïveté of Holden Caulfield produces a bittersweet humor in Salinger's novel.]

The literalness and innocence of Holden's point of view in the face of the tremendously complicated and often depraved facts of life make for the humor of this novel: serious haggles with belligerent taxi-drivers; abortive conversational attempts with a laconic prostitute in a hurry; an "intellectual" discussion with a pompous and phony intellectual only a few years older than himself; an expedition with Sally Hayes, which is one of the funniest expeditions, surely, in the history of juvenilia. Holden's contacts with the outside world are generally extremely funny. It is his self-communings that are tragic and touching—a dark whirlpool churning fiercely below the unflagging hilarity of his surface activities. Holden's difficulties affect his nervous system but never his vision. It is the vision of an innocent. To the lifeline of this vision he clings invincibly, as he does to a phonograph record he buys for Phoebe (till it breaks) and a red hunting cap that is dear to him and that he finally gives to Phoebe, and to Allie's baseball glove. He has a hunger for stability. He loves the Museum of Natural History because the figures in the glass cases don't change; no matter how often you go, the Eskimo is still there catching fish, the deer drinking out of the water hole, the squaw weaving the same blanket. You change the circumstances of your visit—you have an overcoat on one time when you didn't before, or you may have "passed by one of those puddles in the street with gasoline rainbows in them," but the squaw and the deer and the Eskimo are stable. (It was the reason Keats liked the suspended attitudes of the figures on the Grecian urn.) Holden knows things won't remain the same; they are dissolving, and he cannot reconcile himself to it. He hasn't the knowledge to trace the process of dissolution or the mental clarity to define it; all he knows is that he is gasping in the avalanche of disintegration around him. And yet there is an exhilaration, an immense relief in the final scene of this novel, at the Central Park carrousel with Phoebe. ("I felt so damn happy all of a sudden, the way old Phoebe kept going around and around.") Holden will be all right. One day, he will probably find himself in the mood to call up Jane. He will even become more tolerant of phonies—it is part of the mechanics of living—as he has already had to endure the agony of saying "Glad to've met you" to people he isn't glad to have met. He may even, someday, write a novel. I would like to read it. I loved *this* one. I mean it—I really did.

  —S. N. Behrman, "The Vision of the Innocent," *New Yorker,*
  11 August 1951, pp. 75–76

ERNEST JONES ON HOLDEN'S ALIENATION FROM SOCIETY

[Ernest Jones (1879–1958) was a disciple of Sigmund Freud and author of a definitive biography, *The Life and Work of Sigmund Freud* (1953–57; 3 vols.), as well as other writings on psychoanalysis. In this review, Jones stresses that Holden Caulfield's alienation from society is evocative of every person's emotional difficulties.]

Holden Caulfield is friendly, "democratic," well-bred, and snobbish in ways peculiar to adolescence. He has the beginnings of taste; "corny" is a term frequent in his speech. A virgin, he never knows exactly what any girl may be expecting of him and is afraid to make love to the prostitute supplied by an obliging bellhop. He mistakes whatever is spontaneous in his behavior for madness: "But I'm crazy. I swear to God I am"; if he acts on impulse he feels guilty, though also boastful: "I'm the most terrific liar you ever saw in your life." Bravado and buffoonery imperfectly disguise his conviction of madness and guilt.

His sense of alienation is almost complete—from parents, from friends, from society in general as represented by the prep school from which he has been expelled and the night-club and hotel world of New York in which he endures a week-end exile while hiding out from his family. With his alienation go assorted hatreds—of the movies, of night clubs, of social and intellectual pretension, and so on. And physical disgust: pimples, sex, an old man picking his nose are all equally cause for nausea. It is of little importance that the alienation, the hatreds, and the disgust are those of a sixteen-year-old. Any reader, sharing or remembering something like them, will agree with the conclusion to be drawn from this unhappy odyssey: to borrow a line from Auden, "We must love one another or die." After every other human being has failed him, Caulfield still has his loving ten-year-old sister to love; she embodies the innocence we all hope we have preserved and the wisdom we all hope we have acquired.

The skill with which all this has been worked into 277 pages is most ingenious. But as it proceeds on its insights, which are not really insights since they are so general, *The Catcher in the Rye* becomes more and more a case history of all of us. Radically this writing depends on the reader's recollection of merely similar difficulties; the unique crisis and the unique anguish are not re-created. These emotional ups and downs become increasingly factitious—so much must be included to elicit memories of so many callow heartbreaks—and though always lively in its parts, the book as a whole is predictable and boring.

—Ernest Jones, "Case History of All of Us," *Nation,* 1 September 1951, p. 76

JOHN W. ALDRIDGE ON HOLDEN'S CONTEMPT FOR THE
WORLD

[John W. Aldridge (b. 1922), a former professor of
English at the University of Michigan, is a widely published critic and author of *After the Lost Generation*
(1951) and *In the Country of the Young* (1970), a study
of American youth. In this extract, Aldridge points out
a fundamental difference between Holden Caulfield
and Huck Finn in that Holden has a deep-seated contempt for the world that hinders his maturity.]

Mr. Salinger's *The Catcher in the Rye,* like *Adventures of
Huckleberry Finn,* is a study in the spiritual picaresque, the jour-
ney that for the young is all one way, from holy innocence to
such knowledge as the world offers, from the reality which illusion demands and thinks it sees to the illusion which reality
insists, at the point of madness, we settle for. But the great difference between the two novels is the measure not merely of
the change in time and history of a cultural situation, but of the
changed moral circumstances in which innocence typically
finds itself in crisis and lends itself to drama. The innocence of
Huckleberry Finn is a compound of frontier ignorance, juvenile
delinquency, and penny-dreadful heroism. It begs for the challenge of thugs, thieves, swindlers, and feuds, and that is what
it gets and delights in, takes such delight in, in fact, that even
when the dangers become real and the escapes increasingly
narrow, we know it is all in fun, that this is innocence living out
its concocted daydream of glory in which no one really gets
hurt, and even the corpses climb to their feet and dust themselves off at dinnertime. Still, in the suspension of our disbelief,
in the planned illusion of the novel itself, the innocence and the
world of violence appear to be seriously and effectively
opposed. The innocence is the raft to which Huck and Jim, in
flight from the dangers of the shore, make their narrow
escapes. It is the river itself, time, faith, continuity, moving
endlessly and dependably beside and between the temporary
and futile altercations of men. And it is the raft and the river
together which give the innocence of *Huckleberry Finn* its focus
and breadth of implication, so that it exists at once on the level

of naïveté at which it responds to adventure and on the level of maturity at which it lends itself to allegory.

The innocence of Mr. Salinger's Holden Caulfield, on the other hand, is a compound of urban intelligence, juvenile contempt, and *New Yorker* sentimentalism, and the only challenge it begs for, the only challenge it has left to beg for, is the challenge of the genuine, the truly human, in a world which has lost both the means of adventure and the means of love. But it is in the nature of Holden's dilemma, his spiritual confinement in this world, that he lacks a concrete basis, can find no concrete embodiment, for the ideal against which he judges, and finds wanting, the life around him. He has objects for his contempt but no objects other than his sister for his love—no raft, no river, no Jim, and no Tom. He is forced, consequently, simply to register his contempt, his developing disillusionment; and it is inevitable that he should seem after a time to be registering it in a vacuum, for just as he can find no concrete equivalent in life for the ideal which he wishes life to embody, so the persons on whom he registers his contempt seem inadequate to it and unjustly accused by it. The boorish prep school roommate, the hypocritical teacher, the stupid women in the Lavender Room, the resentful prostitute, the conventional girl friend, the bewildered cab driver, the affected young man at the theater, the old friend who reveals that his interest in Holden is homosexual—these people are all truly objectionable and deserve the places Holden assigns them in his secret hierarchy of class with its categories of phonies, bores, deceivers, and perverts. But they are nonetheless human, albeit dehumanized, and constitute a fair average of what the culture affords. They are part of the truth which Holden does not see and, as it turns out, is never able to see—that this is what one part of humanity *is*; the lies, the phoniness, the hypocrisy are the compromises which innocence is forced by the world to make. This is the reality on which Holden's illusion is finally broken, but no recognition follows, and no conversion. He remains at the end what he was at the beginning—cynical, defiant, and blind. And as for ourselves, there is identification but no insight, a sense of pathos but not of tragedy. It may be that Mr. Salinger made the most of his subject, but his subject was not adequate to his intention, just as Holden's world is not adequate to his contempt, and that is probably because it does not possess sufficient humanity to make the search for humanity dramatically feasible.

—John W. Aldridge, "The Society of Three Novels," *In Search of Heresy: American Literature in an Age of Conformity* (New York: McGraw-Hill, 1956), pp. 129–31

CHARLES H. KEGEL ON COMMUNICATION IN *THE CATCHER IN THE RYE*

[Charles H. Kegel (b. 1924) is a former professor of English at Idaho State University and coauthor of *Communication: Principles and Practice* (1959). In this extract, Kegel believes that Holden Caulfield's difficulties derive from an inability to communicate with others, which is itself a product of his hatred of "phoniness."]

⟨. . .⟩ the main reason for Caulfield's communicative difficulty lies in his absolute hatred of phoniness. And he finds that phoniness, that hypocrisy, not only in the world of his personal contacts, but in the world of art as well. He detests phony books, phony music, phony movies and plays. He sees Hamlet as a "sad, screwed-up type guy" and wants him played that way instead of "like a goddam general." Likewise he is bothered by the way people "clap for the wrong things" and hence corrupt the promising artist. Very poignantly he understands the plight of Ernie, the piano player, or of brother D.B., once a sincere writer, but now "out in Hollywood . . . being a prostitute." He wants more Thomas Hardys—"old Thomas Hardy" Caulfield calls him endearingly—because he knows that the creator of "old Eustacia Vye" refused to prostitute himself, refused to be phony.

Holden Caulfield's inability to communicate satisfactorily with others represents itself symbolically in the uncompleted telephone calls and undelivered messages which permeate the novel. Seeing a phone booth is almost more than he can stand, for he almost constantly feels like "giving somebody a buzz." On fifteen separate occasions he gets the urge to communicate by phone, yet only four calls are completed, and those with unfortunate results. Usually the urge dies without his having even attempted to place the call; he seems fearful of what the results will be and rationalizes, "I wasn't in the mood." Likewise, none of the several verbal messages he asks others to deliver for him gets through to the intended receiver; he simply cannot succeed in making contact.

Growing logically out of this prolonged incommunicability is Caulfield's intention to become a deaf-mute. So repulsed is he by the phoniness around him that he despairs of communicating with anybody, and in a passage fraught with import, he contemplates a retreat within himself.

> I figured I could get a job at a filling station somewhere, putting gas and oil in people's cars. I didn't care what kind of a job it was, though. Just so people didn't know me and I didn't know anybody. I thought what I'd do was, I'd pretend I was one of those deaf-mutes. That way I wouldn't have any goddam stupid useless conversations with anybody. If anybody wanted to tell me something, they'd have to write it on a piece of paper and shove it over to me. They'd get bored as hell doing that after a while, and then I'd be through with having conversations for the rest of my life. Everybody'd think I was just a poor deaf-mute bastard and they'd leave me alone. . . . I'd cook all my own food, and later on, if I wanted to get married or something, I'd meet this beautiful girl that was also a deaf-mute and we'd get married. She'd come to live in my cabin with me, and if she wanted to say anything to me, she'd have to write it on a goddam piece of paper, like everybody else.

Significantly, the fact that a message does get through to Phoebe—the only successful communication in the entire novel—leads toward the abandonment of the deaf-mute retreat. The Rousseauistic-Wordsworthian theme of childhood innocence and sincerity which Salinger had played upon so effectively in "For Esmé—with Love and Squalor" works its magic again. It is Phoebe who furnishes the clue to the solution of his problem, and when he refuses to ride the carrousel with her and thus gives up his idealistic attempts "to grab for the gold ring," he has initiated his transition from adolescence to adulthood. He does not, of course, capitulate to the phoniness of life, but he attains an attitude of tolerance, understanding, and love which will make it endurable. There can be no doubt that when he returns to New York—for he, unlike Dedalus, will return home—he will be in the mood to give "old Jane a buzz."

—Charles H. Kegel, "Incommunicability in Salinger's *Catcher in the Rye*," *Western Humanities Review* 11, No. 1 (Winter 1957): 189–90

WILLIAM FAULKNER ON HOLDEN AS AN ANACHRONISM

[William Faulkner (1897–1962) is perhaps the most distinguished American novelist of the first half of the twentieth century and the author of such major works as *The Sound and the Fury* (1929), *As I Lay Dying* (1930), and *Light in August* (1932). In this extract— taken from a question-and-answer session when Faulkner was writer-in-residence at the University of Virginia in 1957–58—Faulkner maintains that Holden was a kind of anachronism in his own time, a young man whose innocence and sensitivity were becoming increasingly rare in his generation.]

⟨April 24, 1958:⟩

Q. I've sometimes thought that the tragedy of Holden Caulfield was that he did not fall, in a way. That if he fell off into humanity he might have found it.

A. Well, he would have to have been tougher than he was. If he had been tougher than that there wouldn't have been any story in the first place. But his story was an intelligent, very sensitive young man who was—in this day and time was an anachronism, was almost an obsolescence, trying to cope with a struggle with the present-day world which he was not fitted for, when he didn't want money, he didn't want position, anything, he just wanted to find man and wanted something to love, and he couldn't. There was nothing there. The nearest he

came to it was his sister who was a child and though she tried
to love him she couldn't understand his problem. The only
other human beings he ran into he had preconceptions to
doubt—the teacher which could have helped him, and he sud-
denly began to suspect the teacher's motives.

—William Faulkner, *Faulkner in the University: Class Conferences
at the University of Virginia 1957–1958*, ed. Frederick L. Gwynn
and Joseph L. Blotner (Charlottesville: University Press of
Virginia, 1959), pp. 246–47

❧

FREDERICK L. GWYNN AND JOSEPH L. BLOTNER ON HOLDEN AND JESUS CHRIST

[Frederick L. Gwynn (b. 1916) is the author of *Sturge
Moore and the Life of Art* (1951) and coeditor of *The
Case for Poetry* (1954). Joseph L. Blotner (b. 1923), a
leading scholar on William Faulkner and author of
Faulkner: A Biography (1966), is a former professor of
English at the University of Michigan. In this extract,
Gwynn and Blotner emphasize the parallels between
Holden Caulfield and Jesus Christ, especially their self-
sacrifice and their love of others.]

This novel's exciting resemblances to *Adventures of
Huckleberry Finn* have been justly noted by a number of critics—the comic irony, the colloquial language, the picaresque
structure, and the theme of anti-phoniness—and it is not incon-
ceivable that some day Holden Caulfield may be as well known
an American boy as Huck Finn. For a reader goes through much
the same pattern of relishing both boys: first it is the release
provided by their rebellion against society, then the inspiration
of their honesty against sham, and then the sympathetic awareness of their melancholy roles. After the reader recovers from
the releasing joy of Holden's invective (e.g., "Her son was
doubtless the biggest bastard that ever went to Pencey, in the
whole crumby history of the school") and of his exposure of
phoniness (e.g., a Radio City Christmas complete with what has

been identified as the movie of James Hilton's *Random Harvest*), he goes on to appreciate the pathos of Holden's loneliness and frustration.

But nervous cynicism and neurosis are not enough for fiction in depth, and the next step for a reader should be to realize that Holden Caulfield is actually a saintly Christian person (there is no need to call him a Christ-figure). True, he has little notion of the love of God, and he thinks that "all the children in our family are atheists." But (1) he himself never does a wrong thing: instead of commandments, Holden breaks only garage windows (when his brother dies) and the no-smoking rule in the Pencey dormitory. (2) He sacrifices himself in a constant war against evil, even though he has a poignantly Manichean awareness of its ubiquity ("If you had a million years to do it in, you couldn't rub out even *half* the [ubiquitously scrawled dirty words] in the world.") And most important, (3) his reward is to understand that if one considers humanity, one must love it. The text for Holden's behavior is his insistence—oddly enough, to his Quaker friend Childs on absolute primitive Christianity: "Jesus never sent old Judas to Hell. . . . I think any one of the Dis*cip*les would've sent him to Hell and all—and fast, too—but I'll bet anything Jesus didn't do it."

For Jesus and Holden Caulfield truly love their neighbors, especially the poor in goods, appearance, and spirit. Holden not only gives ten dollars to the nuns in the station but also he is depressed by their meagre breakfast and the fact that they will never be "going anywhere swanky for lunch." He worries about where the ducks in Central Park can go when the water freezes, and how wretched his mother would feel if he died— "because she still isn't over my brother Allie yet." He is kind to the repulsive Ackley, with his "Sinus trouble, pimples, lousy teeth, halitosis, crumby fingernails," and he tries to obviate Slagle's envy of his Mark Cross luggage. Most significantly, for an adolescent undergoing the torturing growing pains of sex, he sympathizes with the girl's situation—with the ugly daughter of Pencey's headmaster, with both the ugly girl and the beautiful girl in the nightclub undergoing male treatment from their escorts, with the prostitute Sunny, with the girl whom Luce has enjoyed and now derogates, and especially with Jane Gallagher, the girl whose fear Holden appreciates (she wouldn't move her checker kings out of the back row) and whose virtue he fears Stradlater has taken. And like Jesus with his Judas, he still forgives Stradlater and the bellboy Maurice who have betrayed and beaten him. Indeed, this is the old-fashioned moral, stated haltingly at the very end by Holden Caulfield, who wishes to be the Catcher in the Rye suffering little children to come to him and be saved from falling over the cliff. He puts it this way: "About all I know is, I sort of *miss* everybody I told about. Even old Stradlater and Ackley, for instance. I think I even miss that goddam Maurice. It's funny. Don't ever tell anybody anything. If you do, you start missing everybody." In less concrete words: If you are aware of the human comedy, you must love individual human beings. The ending of *The Catcher in the Rye* is just as artistically weak—and as humanly satisfying—as that of *Huckleberry Finn*.

—Frederick L. Gwynn and Joseph L. Blotner, "*The Catcher in the Rye* (1951), *The Fiction of J. D. Salinger* (Pittsburgh: University of Pittsburgh Press, 1958), pp. 28–31

CHRISTOPHER PARKER ON THE APPEAL OF *THE CATCHER IN THE RYE* TO YOUNG PEOPLE

[Christopher Parker (b. 1942), who at the time he wrote this essay was an undergraduate at Oberlin College, offers a personal view of why *The Catcher in the Rye,* and especially the figure of Holden Caulfield, is of such appeal to young people. Parker finds Holden sincere, uncompromising, and engagingly inconsistent.]

So what was Caulfield's problem—if he had one. He'd met a dilemma—like all the rest of us; he didn't give in and he didn't ignore (like most of the rest of us). And he couldn't find any other solution except good old Phoebe on the carrousel. You could say he was trying to find himself, his identity, and all that; but that's a lot of categorical nonsense—who isn't? It's evident that he was also fed up with hypocrisy—but I think Caulfield's real problem is that he was trying desperately to be sincere in an insincere world, with FUCK YOU signs on the walls of children's corridors, wheezing bald caddy-driving alumni who want to find their initials carved in the door of the can, Antolinis who have the answers but don't use them, and Mr. Vinsons who yell "Digression!" at you every time you become excited enough in an idea you have to forget about the classroom exercise and start talking about the idea. Caulfield was outside of himself looking for others. He wasn't a critical smart-aleck—far, far from it. I'm not trying to say that Caulfield's way is right and society's is wrong—but I do think that Caulfield, the individual, is far more human and right than those of us on the outside asking him if he's going to apply himself or not.

The good thing about Caulfield is that he's trying to do it all by himself—no Beatnik—no Bohemian—no Ivy League—just Holden Caulfield. He knows the others are just as phony as the "American Dream," and he also knows that he's being a bit of a phony; he realizes he's in a bad way but he doesn't know what to do about it.

Why do I like *The Catcher?* Because it puts forth in a fairly good argument the problems which boys of my age face, and also perhaps the inadequacy with which some of us attempt to cope with them. I have great admiration for Caulfield because he didn't compromise. I think he was relatively free of self-worship—his cause was certainly justified, if not just. I think Salinger deals fairly with him—he gives enough grounds to argue either pro or con. Some people condemn Caulfield as "not liking anything," but he does—he likes the only things really worth liking, whereas most of us like all the things that aren't worth liking. Because he is sincere he won't settle for less.

I think most fellows who read *The Catcher* don't think about it enough—what's really behind it all. They think he's a cool guy, so they imitate his casual talk and nonchalant attitude. Salinger didn't invent the talk, nor Holden Caulfield for that matter, but it's certainly become much more popular since. I don't even think most fellows notice it's called the "*Catcher* in the Rye" when in the song it's really supposed to be "meet a body," not "catch a body."

I can feel every impulse and emotion that Caulfield experiences—and he's by no means consistent. Sometimes he does exactly what he calls phony in another. That's why I think the book is good—it shows the dilemma of needing people and yet not wanting them. For instance, as Caulfield says after he's asked Sally (whom he despises) to go for a trip and she refuses: "The terrible part, though, is that I *meant* it when I asked her. That's the terrible part. I swear to God I'm a madman." He cannot break completely away from what he knows is phony. Does he make an effort to get along? I certainly think he does, but when it comes to the point of getting along or going phony, he sacrifices the first and ends up with Stradlater's fist in his mouth. The idiot Stradlater stays in school and Caulfield gets the ax—and it's not because he's lazy—he does it deliberately—because he just can't do stupid things like describing a room. Rather he describes his brother Allie's baseball mitt with poetry written on it. If he were unintelligent, there would have been no problem. It is because he was really looking, sincerely, for a pure thing outside himself, that I admire him.

Hope I gave a crazy kid's view of a crazy kid.

—Christopher Parker, " 'Why the Hell *Not* Smash All the Windows?,' " *Salinger: A Critical and Personal Portrait,* ed. Henry Anatole Grunwald (New York: Harper & Brothers, 1962), pp. 257–58

ALFRED CHESTER ON SALINGER'S CHARACTERIZATION

[Alfred Chester (1928–1971) wrote a novel, *The Exquisite Corpse* (1967) and a short story collection, *Behold Goliath* (1965), and his essays and reviews were collected in *Looking for Genet* (1992). In this article, Chester discusses Salinger's portrayals of character, asserting that Salinger is best in his depiction of types.]

The genius or, if you will, ingenuity, of Salinger's earlier work lay not in his creation of individuals, but in his depiction of types. Nearly everyone in his stories and in his novel rang bells like mad. You could not have learned to know thyself better from reading his work, but you might have recognized some of your sillier traits, and you would definitely have recognized the people and the things around you in it. He was always putting his finger on just the right gesture, on the precise tone of voice, on the exact object or circumstance. And if one suspected that he was in scorn of the vanities and trivialities of the milieu he described, he made them nevertheless glamorous, or rather he did not subtract from metropolitan life any of its mythical and publicized glamor. From *The Catcher* one came away charmed by the very things that appalled Holden: the night-club, the theater, the pretentious sophisticates, the stupid office girls, the prep school, everything. It was all so precisely depicted that it gave one the pleasure of the miniature. You couldn't possibly be offended by it—even if you happened to be a stupid and pretentious night-club. *The Catcher* is, so far as I know, an unparalleled example of a writer's having the best of both worlds, of getting both God and Mammon to work for him wholeheartedly. (I'm not trying to diminish the value of *The Catcher* which—though both it and I have grown twelve years staler—is still one of the freshest novels this country has produced since the war.) The life in *The Catcher,* like the life in some of the *Nine Stories*—since whose appearance I have grown ten years staler, while they have grown a generation staler—springs from the swift, immediate, authentic response of the characters to the world around them. And the intense charm of the books came from the fact that his characters were responding to *our* world which also happened to be theirs. Their world will go as soon as our world goes (and then, of course, the charm will disappear, as it already has from Esmé, from Teddy, from most of them) because it was never transmuted; it was merely depicted. What once was the most moving scene in *The Catcher*—when Holden tries to explain his anguish over American civilization to the absurd girl he's with at Rockefeller Center—has now become flat and insufficient. The time for disgust over Cadillacs has passed and Holden's suffering does not seem interesting or real enough, enough *itself,* to make us separate it from its object, thereby turning the object into symbol and the suffering into our own. All his lament makes us want to do is prod him gently, wake him up, and say: nobody cares about Cadillacs any more.

—Alfred Chester, "Salinger: How to Love without Love," *Commentary* 35, No. 6 (June 1963): 467–68

JONATHAN BAUMBACH ON HOLDEN AS A SECULAR SAINT

[Jonathan Baumbach (b. 1933) is a widely published novelist and short story writer and author of a critical study, *The Landscape of Nightmare: Studies in the Contemporary American Novel* (1965). He is a member of the board of directors of the Teachers and Writers Collaborative. In this extract, Baumbach believes that Holden's distinctiveness comes from his wish to be a secular saint—to be both innocent and sophisticated.]

Like all of Salinger's fiction, *The Catcher in the Rye* is not only *about* innocence, it is actively *for* innocence, as if retaining one's childness were an existential possibility. The metaphor of the title—Holden's fantasy vision of standing in front of a cliff and protecting playing children from falling (Falling)—is, despite the impossibility of its realization, the only positive action affirmed in the novel. It is, in Salinger's Manichean universe of child angels and adult "phonies," the only moral alternative; otherwise all is corruption. And since to prevent the Fall is a spiritual as well as physical impossibility, Salinger's idealistic heroes are doomed to either suicide (Seymour) or insanity (Holden, Sergeant X) or mysticism (Franny); or to moral dissolution (Eloise, D. B., Mr. Antolini)—the way of the world. In Salinger's finely honed prose, at once idiomatically real and poetically stylized, we get the terms of Holden's ideal adult occupation.

> Anyway, I kept picturing all these little kids playing some game in this big field of rye and all. Thousands of little kids, and nobody's around—nobody big, I mean—except me. And I'm standing on the edge of some crazy cliff. What I have to do, I have to catch everybody if they start to go over the cliff—I

mean if they're running and they don't look where they're going. I have to come out from somewhere and *catch* them. That's all I'd do all day. I'd just be the catcher in the rye and all. I know it's crazy, but that's the only thing I'd really like to be.

Apparently Holden's wish is purely selfless. What he wants, in effect, is to be a saint—the protector and savior of innocence. But what he also wants—for he is still one of the running children himself—is that someone prevent *his* fall. This is his paradox; he must leave innocence to protect innocence. At sixteen he is ready to shed his innocence and move like Adam into the fallen adult world, but he resists because those who are no longer innocent seem to him foolish as well as corrupt. In a sense, then, he is looking for an exemplar, a wise and good father whose example will justify his own initiation into manhood. Before Holden can become a catcher in the rye, he must find another catcher in the rye to show him how it is done.

—Jonathan Baumbach, "The Saint as a Young Man: A Reappraisal of *The Catcher in the Rye*," *Modern Language Quarterly* 25, No. 4 (December 1964): 462–64

ROBERT P. MOORE ON PURITANICAL CRITICISMS OF *THE CATCHER IN THE RYE*

[Robert P. Moore is former chairman of the department of English at St. John's High School in Houston, Texas. In this extract, Moore combats the beliefs of many who believe that *The Catcher in the Rye* is objectionable in its negativity and its use of profanity, claiming that these qualities are part of the novel's realistic portrayal of modern youth.]

The usual charge made against Salinger's *Catcher in the Rye,* which may well be one of the most controversial books of our time, is that it is a dirty book. It includes four letter words that, some suppose, the adolescent in America is being introduced to for the first time. It includes dirty scenes in hotel rooms, and it includes crude and violent scenes in dormitory rooms.

Another charge is that, like *Adventures of Huckleberry Finn*, it is a negative, subversive, and immoral book. Holden Caulfield rejects his school, and the school rejects him. Holden is without ambition, without creed, without purpose. He is a drifter, a wanderer, an adventurer who seeks not adventure but smut and the negative satisfactions of a negative rebellion.

And, of course, in a very inaccurate and superficial sense, to the unseeing, unperceptive, and puritanical eye, much of this is not without foundation. There is negation in the book, and there is dirt and crudeness and subversion and immorality. But it is the world around Holden Caulfield that is negative. It is the world around Holden Caulfield that writes the dirty words on the walls, that does the crude things that make the sensitive cringe, that is immoral and duplicitous and vengeful. The world around Holden but never Holden himself.

The point central to the novel is that Holden is the innocent youth in a world of cruel and hypocritical adults. He is the twentieth-century, unromantic version of Melville's Billy Budd. He is the knight-errant trying to make some sense, find some meaning, gain some understanding of a world that won't listen to him, a world that doesn't care, a world that segregates the sixteen-year-old, separate and never, never equal, a blind, callous, fumbling, bumbling world that often reduces him to tears.
—Robert P. Moore, "The World of Holden," *English Journal* 54, No. 3 (March 1965): 159

BERNARD C. KINNICK ON HOLDEN'S IDEALISM

[Bernard C. Kinnick is a former professor of English at Colorado State College. In this extract, Kinnick believes that it is Holden Caulfield's idealism—his refusal to accept the status quo—that is the most valuable aspect of Salinger's novel.]

Many adults feel that the adolescent (characterized here by Holden Caulfield) should "grow up," accept the world for what it is, and live in it. In essence, throw off any ideas of ever reaching for or becoming a part of an ideal world. At first notice, this is a sound but conservative recommendation. However, taken seriously and logically, the advice would put an end to any search for idealism, sincerity, and decency. True, it is the kind of advice that most are forced to give sooner or later—and to take. But, is it not possible that there are some adolescents (and adults) who are simply not like the majority, who cannot accept the human condition for what it is, who cannot resign themselves to the existence of injustice, ugliness, and pain? This refusal to accept the status quo in the world marks not only the adolescents—it also marks many adults who may be seen as an adolescent who has refused to "grow up," who is unable or unwilling to cover his inner life with the calluses necessary for the ordinary life. These individuals wage war with the-way-things-are. They are martyrs in the eternal search for idealism. Holden Caulfield, if he is a rebel at all, is a rebel against the human condition and as such he deserves his small share of nobility.

It is most important to protect and cherish the uniqueness of the adolescent who, rightly or wrongly, refuses to accept completely the existing reality of the adult world. Resistance to the world is not bad or evil in itself—rather, it may be that one thing that gives the adolescent his uniqueness as a human being. The continuous search of the adolescent for a semi-Utopian world where truth, beauty, and goodness would abound must be encouraged rather than stamped upon. Holden, like most adolescents, continues in an urgent pace to search for his true self and his place in the world. The adolescent's disillusionment and sense of failure arrive when his search for an ideal and decent world for his ideal and decent self to respond to, proves useless. Thus, the adolescent's rebellion is in part a protest against the ugly world transmitted to him and in part a sort of punishment for the world's lack of idealism.

A great part of the adolescent's idealism probably stems from his resistance to growing up. Still, it is rather difficult to criticize this resistance to entering a world lacking in the ideals found within the spirit of the young adolescent. Holden's distaste for his findings, in his collision with the outside world, seem to be warranted. If this be true, one should recognize the adolescent's need for viewing and experiencing himself from the inside—exploring his inner life where idealism and notions of Utopia are free to live and flourish. As reality closes in on the adolescent, he fights all the harder to escape it and preserve his vision of Utopia or self-made paradise. (Perhaps in cherishing the world of the adolescent, we cherish ourselves, or, rather, the memory of ourselves in youth. We admire what we once were, or think we were, or wanted to become.)

Adolescent idealism is found in Holden's quest for sincerity, for honesty between people. His repeated insistence, "I mean it, I really do," gives credence to this search. And when Holden does experience decency, as he does with his sister Phoebe, he reacts decently to it. Holden, as many adolescents, is extremely sensitive to the good and evil in society. He may often be criticized for being too sensitive about the realities of society to live in it. But might not the opposite be true? Perhaps the adolescent is too sensitive to ignore it, to look the other way, to withdraw, as the so-called well-adjusted and busy adults withdraw into their protective shells when faced with society's terrors and ugliness. Holden simply cannot accept the injustices, the ugliness, the lovelessness that surround him. He meets them head-on. It is to the adolescent's great credit that, in spite of numerous disillusionments, he stubbornly clings to his conviction that there *must* be a hidden core of sincerity somewhere among the world's hypocrisies. As long as the adolescent can hold on to the conviction that there are external counterparts to his ideal self, he can keep going. When this vision of his self-made Utopia is finally broken in his encounter with the world of reality, the adolescent must compromise or painfully withdraw in one of many ways from this same world of reality.

The idealistic rebellion of adolescence is a good thing when it is harnessed to idealistic and Utopian schemes, even though unworkable in the hard world of practicality. There *must* be some virtue in rebellion against a false, lying, and deceitful society. Most adolescents eventually come to terms with things as they are. They give up their Utopian and idealistic ideas of working any radical changes in the social structure or in the culture's value system. They try at least, painful as it may be, to find their own "realistic" place in society. Holden was unable to do this very thing. For this, he is both intensely praised and violently condemned.

Is Holden Caulfield an outsider in this world, or is he really an insider with the track all to himself?

—Bernard C. Kinnick, "Holden Caulfield: Adolescents' Enduring Model," *High School Journal* 53, No. 8 (May 1970): 441–43

DUANE EDWARDS ON THE FLAWS IN HOLDEN'S CHARACTER

[Duane Edwards is a professor of English at Fairleigh Dickinson University (Madison, NJ) and the author of several critical articles on American literature. In this extract, Edwards maintains that many critics have idealized Holden and failed to realize his flaws—his refusal to accept responsibility for his actions, his inconsistencies, and his sexual problems.]

When Holden says that he wants to be the catcher in the rye, he reveals a great deal about himself—a great deal more than he knows. He reveals that he does not seriously want to learn about himself. He simply won't make the effort. After all, he hasn't bothered to read Burns's poem; he isn't even able to quote accurately the one line he heard a small boy recite; he doesn't know that Burns's narrator contemplates kissing the "body" he meets in the rye field. So when Holden changes the word "meet" to "catch" and talks not of love but of potential death (falling off a cliff), he reveals his willingness to distort the truth by ignoring—or even changing—the facts. He also reveals his use of displacement: he substitutes one response for another. He focuses on danger and potential death instead of love and a personal relationship. Ultimately, he reveals his unreliability as the narrator of his own life's story.

Fortunately, the fact that Holden distorts doesn't matter to anyone concerned with the *significance* of the events and dialogue recorded in *The Catcher in the Rye.* Like the psychoanalyst analyzing a dream, the reader can analyze what matters most: the distortions. What emerges from this analysis is an awareness that Salinger's narrator is ironic: he doesn't understand (or know) himself, but he unwittingly lets the reader know what he is like. In fact, he does so at the very beginning of the novel when he promises to give the reader none of "that David Copperfield kind of crap" about his "lousy childhood." Normally, such a statement would be innocent and unrevealing, but Holden isn't "normal": he's a severely depressed adolescent telling the story of his youth while in a mental institution. He is, by his own admission, sick. So his refusal to talk about the incidents of his childhood signifies that he will remain ill, as does his chilling advice, "Don't ever tell anybody anything," at the end of the novel.

Elsewhere in the novel there is evidence that Holden will remain ill because he refuses to assume responsibility for his own actions. For example, when he is "the goddam manager of the fencing team," he leaves the "foils and equipment and stuff" on the subway. Although he admits that he left them there, he hastens to add: "It wasn't all my fault." Here and elsewhere he simply will not or can not let his mind rest without ambivalence or qualification on a conclusion.

Ambivalence is, in fact, characteristic of Holden and the surest evidence of his mental instability. If he loathes what he loves and does so intensely, he is by no means well. He is also not what he and many readers assume he is: an anti-establishment figure whose disgust is directed entirely at other people.

It's easy to demonstrate that Holden is ambivalent since he is ambivalent toward so many people and things. He hates movies and the Lunts but attends movies and takes Sally to a play starring the Lunts. He is contemptuous of Pencey but is careful to emphasize that it has a "very good academic rating." He claims to loathe the perverts he sees through his hotel window but makes a special effort to watch them and even admits that "that kind of junk is sort of fascinating" and that he wouldn't mind doing it himself "if the opportunity came up." He criticizes phony conversations but engages in them himself—with Mr. Spencer and Ernest Morrow's mother, for example. He criticizes "old Spencer" (and others) for using a phony word like "grand," but he himself uses equally phony words such as "nice" and "swell." He loathes Ackley and Stradlater but misses them as soon as they're gone. He wants to see people—Mr. Antolini, Mr. Spencer, and Carl Luce, for example—but doesn't like them when they're in his presence. Obviously, then, Holden is ambivalent, and ambivalence is a certain indication of mental instability.

What is Holden's problem? Whatever it is in specific form, it's reflected in his inability to relate sexually to females. Holden himself suggests this when he says, "My sex life stinks." But even when he speaks the truth he fools himself: he believes that he cannot "get really sexy" with girls he doesn't like a lot whereas, in reality, he cannot get sexy with a girl he does like. In fact, what he likes about Jane Gallagher is that a relationship with her will not go beyond the hand-holding stage. In his other attempts to establish connections with girls or women, he fails sexually and, in fact, deliberately avoids both affection and serious sexual advances. He kisses Sally Hayes—but in a cab where the relationship cannot go beyond "horsing around." He consents to have a prostitute sent to his hotel room but asks her to stop when she starts "getting funny. Crude and all," that is, when she proceeds from words to action. Aroused by watching the "perverts" in the hotel, he does call up Faith Cavendish, a woman he has never seen, but at an impossibly late hour and so ensures that she will refuse his request for a date. Clearly, Holden has a problem with females.

—Duane Edwards, " 'Don't Ever Tell Anybody Anything,' " *ELH* 44, No. 3 (Fall 1977): 555–56

KERRY MCSWEENEY ON HOLDEN POISED BETWEEN THE CHILDHOOD AND ADULT WORLDS

[Kerry McSweeney (b. 1941), a professor of English at McGill University in Montreal, is the author of *Four Contemporary Novelists* (1983) and studies of *Moby-*

Dick (1986) and *Invisible Man* (1988). In this extract, McSweeney believes that the secret of Holden Caulfield's appeal lies in the fact that he is poised between the worlds of childhood and adulthood and can offer perspectives on both without being a part of either.]

The only work of Salinger's that has not shrunk with the passage of time is *The Catcher in the Rye*. The macro-subject of Salinger's only novel is that of all his fiction; as Carol and Richard Ohmann say in their provocative 'case study of capitalist criticism' of *Catcher* in the autumn 1976 *Critical Inquiry*, the novel is 'among other things a serious critical mimesis of bourgeois life in the Eastern United States ca. 1950'. The micro-subject is a crisis point in the adolescence of a sensitive and perceptive youth: Holden Caulfield is sixteen when the events in the novel take place; seventeen when he narrates them. The social notation is superb: the expensive prep school with its Ackleys and Stradlaters; the lobby of the Biltmore (the *in* place for dates to meet); the Greenwich Village bar and the equally tony Wicker Bar uptown; the crowd in the theatre lobby at intermission; Mr and Mrs Antolini; the sad 'girls' from Seattle who are in the big city to have a good time; and so on.

Similarly, the macro-theme of *Catcher* is that of the rest of Salinger; the almost Dickensian dichotomy between the lower world of the many and the innocent, constantly threatened world of the few: the dead Allie, who used to write poems all over his baseball mitt, and Jane Gallagher, who when playing checkers always kept her kings in the back row (both activities recall Seymour's admonition not to aim when shooting marbles); the two nuns who 'went around collecting dough in those beat-up old straw baskets'; and Phoebe, the wise child, for love of whom her exhausted brother is moved to tears on the novel's last page.

What is different in *Catcher,* and what must be considered the key to its success, is its method. Holden's first person narration *ipso facto* removes from the novel any trace of *New Yorker* preciosities. Everything is seen from Holden's point of view and reported in his pungent vernacular. The voice and the perceptions are wholly convincing and of sustained freshness.

Indeed, the only comparatively flat scenes—on the train with Morrow's mother, in the restaurant with the nuns—are the two places in the novel where one feels that there is something derivative about Holden's characterisation and narration, that he is drawn more from *Huckleberry Finn* than from life.

Holden's adolescent perspective, halfway between the childhood and adult worlds, fully a part of neither yet acutely sensitive to and observant of both, provides the perfect point of focus for *Catcher*. Holden is in a privileged though precarious position. A two- or three-year difference in his age, in either direction, would have made for an entirely different book. In his own image, to which the novel's title calls attention, Holden is 'on the edge of some crazy cliff', with little kids playing in a field of rye on one side of him, an abyss on the other. Like that of Nick Carraway, Fitzgerald's narrator in *The Great Gatsby,* Holden's bifocal vision allows him simultaneously to register both the phoniness and meretriciousness of the fallen world and the sense of wonder and tenderness, and the supernal *frissons,* of the innocent world. And since they are so well grounded (and thereby authenticated) in a particular person at a particular time of life, Holden's longings, needs and intimations of mystery never become sentimental or merely notional. Indeed they are the most resonant images in all of Salinger of the longing for the absent true life, as in Holden's haunting question of where the Central Park ducks go in the winter, his love for the dead brother, and for the live sister whom he wishes could, like things in the museum, always stay the way she now is and never have to grow up.

Near the end of *Catcher* Holden reflects that there is no place where one is free from somebody sneaking up and writing 'Fuck you' right under your nose. Holden's erasures of this phrase recall the last page of *The Great Gatsby* when Nick Carraway deletes an obscene word from Gatsby's steps before going down to the water's edge to begin meditation on the capacity for wonder and the longing for absent true life, which draws one ceaselessly back into the past. There are more similarities between Fitzgerald's and Salinger's novels (and between the two authors) than might at first meet the eye, and a brief concluding comparison of the two may be of help in making a stab at gauging the 'real' status of *Catcher*.

Both novels turn on the contrast of a fallen world of aggression, selfishness and phoniness and a tenuous higher world of (to use Fitzgerald's phrase) 'heightened sensitivity to the promises of life'. Both writers have been charged with having no real social vision to complement their acute social notation: what the Ohmanns say of Holden Caulfield may, *mutatis mutandis,* be said of his creator: 'for all his perceptiveness . . . he is an adolescent with limited understanding of what he perceives'. And Fitzgerald has of course been described as having been taken in by what he could see through. I believe that this remark is manifestly unfair to Fitzgerald at his best, and that there is much to ponder in his (admittedly oddly phrased) notebook comment that D. H. Lawrence was 'Essential[ly] pre-Marxian. Just as I am essentially Marxian.' There is real social insight in *Gatsby,* which offers a complex anatomy and moral evaluation of the world it describes. Because its bifocal vision is that of a discriminating adult, not that of an engagingly screwed-up teenager, the novel is able to offer a richer and more complex exploration both of the lower world and the higher world of threatened innocence and longing.

—Kerry McSweeney, "Salinger Revisited," *Critical Quarterly* 20, No. 1 (Spring 1978): 66–68

Edwin Haviland Miller on Holden and Allie

[Edwin Haviland Miller (b. 1918) is a former professor of English at New York University and a distinguished critic and biographer. Among his works are *Walt Whitman's Poetry: A Psychological Study* (1969) and *Salem Is My Dwelling Place: A Life of Nathaniel Hawthorne* (1991). In this extract, Miller studies the role of Holden's brother Allie, believing that many of Holden's actions can be gauged as reaction to Allie's death.]

Life stopped for Holden on July 18, 1946, the day his brother died of leukemia. Holden was then thirteen, and four years later—the time of the narrative—he is emotionally still at the same age, although he has matured into a gangly six-foot adolescent. "I was sixteen then," he observes concerning his expulsion from Pencey Prep at Christmas time in 1949, "and I'm seventeen now, and some times I act like I'm about thirteen."

On several occasions Holden comments that his mother has never gotten over Allie's death, which may or may not be an accurate appraisal of Mrs. Caulfield, since the first-person narrative makes it difficult to judge. What we can deduce, though, is that it is an accurate appraisal of Holden's inability to accept loss, and that in his eyes his mother is so preoccupied with Allie that she continues to neglect Holden, as presumably she did when Allie was dying.

The night after Allie's death Holden slept in the garage and broke "all the goddam windows with my fist, just for the hell of it. I even tried to break all the windows on the station wagon we had that summer, but my hand was already broken and everything by that time, and I couldn't do it. It was a very stupid thing to do, I'll admit, but I hardly didn't even know I was doing it, and you didn't know Allie." The act may have been "stupid"—which is one of his pet words to denigrate himself as well as others—but it also reflects his uncontrollable anger, at himself for wishing Allie dead and at his brother for leaving him alone and burdened with feelings of guilt. Similarly, the attack on the station wagon may be seen as his way of getting even with a father who was powerless either to save Allie or to understand Holden. Because he was hospitalized, he was unable to attend the funeral, to witness the completion of the life process, but by injuring himself he received the attention and sympathy which were denied him during Allie's illness. His actions here as elsewhere are inconsistent and ambivalent, but always comprehensible in terms of his reaction to the loss of Allie.

So too is Holden's vocabulary an index to his disturbed emotional state—for all that it might seem to reflect the influence of the movies or his attempts to imitate the diction of his older brother, D.B. At least fifty times, something or somebody *depresses* him—an emotion which he frequently equates with a sense of isolation: "It makes you feel so lonesome and depressed." Although the reiteration of the word reveals the true nature of his state, no one in the novel recognizes the signal, perceiving the boy as a kind of adolescent clown rather than as a seriously troubled youth. As his depression deepens to the point of nervous breakdown, furthermore, Holden—who at some level of awareness realizes that he is falling apart—seeks to obscure the recognition by referring to everything as "crazy" and by facetiously likening himself to a "madman."

"Crap," another word he uses repeatedly, is similarly self-reflexive. Although it is his ultimate term of reductionism for describing the world, like "crazy" it serves to identify another of his projections. He feels dirty and worthless, and so makes the world a reflection of his self-image. Similarly, if he continually asserts, almost screams, that the phony world makes him want to "puke," it is because Holden's world itself has turned to vomit. In his troubled, almost suicidal state he can incorporate nothing, and, worse, he believes there is nothing for him to incorporate. In turn, the significance of his repeated use of variations on the phrase "that killed me" becomes almost self-evident: reflecting his obsession with death, it tells the unsuspecting world that he wishes himself dead, punished and then reunited with Allie.

Although his consistently negative and hostile language thus reflects Holden's despair and is his way of informing the world of his plight, if no one listens it is primarily his own fault. For with the usual fumbling of the hurt he has chosen a means which serves his purposes poorly. While his language may serve to satisfy his need to act out his anger, at the same time it serves to isolate and to punish him further. If in his hostile phrases he is calling for help, he makes certain that he does not receive it. Ashamed of his need—a sixteen-year-old crying for emotional support—and unable to accept kindness since in his guilt he feels he does not deserve it, Holden is locked into his grief and locked out of family and society.

In this respect, the first paragraph of *Catcher in the Rye* is one of the most deceptively revealing possible. Although Holden, the would-be sophisticate, relegates his familial background to "David Copperfield kind of crap," he talks about little else except his "lousy childhood." Arguing that he will not divulge family secrets so as not to cause pain, and pretending to respect the feelings of his parents, he verbally mutilates them, and in an ugly way; but if he is to suffer, so must they. He retaliates in kind, not in kindness. Yet the aggressive, assertive tone masks a pitiful, agonized call for emotional support and love.

—Edwin Haviland Miller, "In Memoriam: Allie Caulfield in *The Catcher in the Rye*," *Mosaic* 15, No. 1 (Winter 1982): 129–31

ALAN NADEL ON *THE CATCHER IN THE RYE* AND THE COLD WAR

[Alan Nadel (b. 1947) is a professor of English at Rensselaer Polytechnic Institute (Troy, NY) and the author of *Invisible Criticism: Ralph Ellison and the American Canon* (1988) and editor of *May All Your Fences Have Gates: Essays on the Drama of August Wilson* (1994). In this extract, Nadel discusses Salinger's novel in the context of the Cold War; in particular, Holden's language reflects such Cold War issues as generalization, the establishment of rules, and the need for authority.]

If, as has been widely noted, *The Catcher in the Rye* owes much to *Adventures of Huckleberry Finn*, it rewrites that classic American text in a world where the ubiquity of rule-governed society leaves no river on which to flee, no western territory for which to light out. The territory is mental, not physical, and Salinger's Huck spends his whole flight searching for raft and river, that is, for the margins of his sanity. A relative term, however, "sanity" merely indicates conformity to a set of norms, and since rhetorical relationships formulate the normative world in which a speaker functions, a fictional text—whether or not it asserts an external reality—unavoidably creates and contains a reality in its rhetorical hierarchies, which are necessarily full of assumptions and negations. This aspect of fiction could not be more emphasized than it is by Holden Caulfield's speech, a speech which, moreover, reflects the pressures and contradictions prevalent in the Cold War society from which it was forged.

An obsessively proscriptive speaker, Caulfield's essay-like rhetorical style—which integrates generalization, specific examples, and consequent rules—prevails throughout the book, subordinating to it most of the description, narration, and dialogue by making them examples in articulating the principles of a rule-governed society. In one paragraph, for example, Caulfield tells us that someone had stolen his coat (example), that Pencey was full of crooks (generalization), and that "the more expensive a school is, the more crooks it has" (rule). In a longer excerpt, from Chapter 9, we can see how the details Caulfield sees from his hotel window—"a man and a woman squirting water out of their mouths at one another"—become examples in a series of generalizations, rules, and consequent evaluations:

> The trouble was, [principle] that kind of junk is sort of fascinating to watch, even if you don't want it to be. For instance, [example] that girl that was getting water squirted all over her face, she was pretty good-looking. I mean that's my big trouble. [generalization] In my *mind,* I'm probably the biggest sex maniac you ever saw. Sometimes [generalization] I can think of *very* crumby stuff I wouldn't mind doing if the opportunity came up. I can even see how it might be quite a lot of fun, [qualification] in a crumby way, and if you were both sort of drunk and all, [more specific example] to get a girl and squirt water or something all over each other's face. The thing is, though, [evaluation] I don't *like* the idea. It [generalization] stinks, if you analyze it. I think [principle arrived at deductively through a series of enthymemes] if you don't really like a girl, you shouldn't horse around with her at all, and if you *do* like her, then you're supposed to like her face, and if you like her face, you ought to be careful about doing crumby stuff to it, [specific application] like squirting water all over it.

Caulfield not only explains his world but also justifies his explanations by locating them in the context of governing rules, rendering his speech not only compulsively explanatory but also authoritarian in that it must demonstrate an authority for *all* his statements, even if he creates that authority merely through rhetorical convention.

With ample space we could list all the rules and principles Caulfield articulates. Here are a few: it's really hard to be roommates with people if your suitcases are better than theirs; "grand" is a phony word; real ugly girls have it tough; people never believe you; seeing old guys in their pajamas and bathrobes is depressing; don't ever tell anybody anything, if you do you start missing everybody. We could easily find scores more, to prove the book a virtual anatomy of social behavior. The book, however, also anatomizes Caulfield's personal behavior: he lies; he has a great capacity for alcohol; he hates to go to bed when he's not even tired; he's very fond of dancing, sometimes; he's a pacifist; he always gets those vomity kind of cabs if he goes anywhere late at night, etc.

As the author of the two anatomies, Caulfield thus manifests two drives: to control his environment by being the one who names and thus creates its rules, and to subordinate the self by being the one whose every action is governed by rules. To put it another way, he is trying to constitute himself both as subject and as object; he is trying to read a social text and to write one. When these two drives come in conflict, there are no options left.

> —Alan Nadel, "Rhetoric, Sanity, and the Cold War: The Significance of Holden Caulfield's Testimony," *Centennial Review* 32, No. 4 (Fall 1988): 351–53

WARREN FRENCH ON HOLDEN AND SOCIOLOGY

[Warren French (b. 1922) is a professor of English at Indiana University-Purdue University at Indianapolis and a prolific literary scholar. Among his books are *John Steinbeck* (1961; rev. 1975), *J. D. Salinger* (1963; rev. 1976), *The Social Novel at the End of an Era* (1966), and *Jack Kerouac* (1986). In this extract, French believes that an understanding of Holden can be achieved by reference to sociological treatises of the time.]

Possible insights into the novel may be gained by turning from the sermons of literary critics to popular sociological speculations about the world that Salinger's novel mirrors.

A much consulted guide to the changing American character during the years of confusion when *Catcher* was published was *The Lonely Crowd* (1950), by David Riesman and Reuel Denney, social scientists at the University of Chicago, and Nathan Glazer, an associate editor of the American Jewish Forum's magazine *Commentary*. Holden Caulfield, however, could not be pigeonholed in any of the three principal categories of personalities explored in the book—tradition-directed (generally passive conformists to established rituals), inner-directed (able to function effectively in society without strict outside controls), and other-directed (controlled by contemporaries, personal friends, or mass media).

In fact, one of the few grounds on which many admirers and detractors of the book can meet is that Holden belongs not to any of the three types, but may be most satisfactorily described as "anomic," which the authors of *The Lonely Crowd* use to mean "ruleless," "ungoverned," "virtually synonymous with maladjusted." A disconcerting problem central to an understanding of the novel arises, however, with the recognition that Holden does not display "the lack of emotion and emptiness of expression" characteristic of "the ambulatory patients in the ward of modern culture," like Seymour Glass and Teddy McArdle, but rather the "hysteria or outlawry . . . characteristic of anomics in the societies depending on earlier forms of direction," as demonstrated by his vehement hatred of institutional confines and his desire to take to the woods in emulation of the mountain men who lived beyond the frontier in early America.

Holden displays remarkable success in resisting the "other-direction" of his "contemporaries," who are the undoing of James Purdy's Malcolm; and, in fact, many readers may admire the novel because Holden is an outsider rather then just another clone. Holden's problems stem from an inner-directed resistance to the regulations of an influential segment of American society whose "keeping-up-with-the-Joneses" life-style has already fossilized into a debilitating tradition. Holden is the victim of the situation that H. L. Mencken characterized with cynical aptness when he described the United States as the only nation that had passed from barbarism to decadence without an intervening flowering of civilization. Holden yearns for the rejuvenating rigors of barbarism while trapped in a reductivist Manhattan society, which has changed only for the worse since Salinger captured its image.

Holden's situation is like that of Ike McCaslin in William Faulkner's "The Bear," when he seeks to reject his heritage of proprietorship to be "initiated" into an earlier culture that allowed people to live closer to nature. (Faulkner, of course, sadly observed that this world was gradually being destroyed by urbanized society, a sentiment that helps account for his sympathy with Salinger's hero, who finds that the human race has disappeared.)

Holden's "deinitiation" is not, however, followed like Ike's by the initiation he seeks, for Holden does not have an experienced tutor like Sam Fathers to direct his induction into his chosen totem. Holden is left entirely to his own devices with no perceptive or experienced adult guidance. Phoebe does wonders for Holden's sagging morale, but she proves more of a handicap than a help to his escape plans by showing him that he is not yet ready to take responsibility for his dreams and that he must move cautiously toward a life-style that may be suited only to himself. She also implies that one must choose for one's self at the age of the traditional initiation into a clan. Holden's hope that Phoebe may still be able to make it in a world that he feels he must reject is indicated by his comment that, when she pleads to run away with him, he hates her most "because she wouldn't be in [her school's] play any more if she went away with me" (268). He simply will not make any compromises; and the only one that he does make at the very end is an agreement with himself not to try to recruit others to his views but to leave them to their own devices. The problem that remains at the end of the book is to what Holden may apply himself: will he indeed have the guts to conduct his isolated vigilante campaign against the "perverty bums" that deface the museums?

What Rosen and James Miller, along with many other critics, have failed to recognize is that Holden does have a vigilante viewpoint—something far from uncommon in the United States. It is somewhat unnerving, in fact, to be scrutinizing his behavior at the time of the tumult over Bernard Goetz, the New Yorker acquitted of shooting four youths who he claimed had harassed him on the subway. *The Catcher in the Rye* remains after three decades a contemporary work because the forces that agitated Holden Caulfield are still active and growing. He could have been tempted to react in the same way as Goetz, if he had the guts (remember his wishing to smash "the perverty bum's" head "on the stone steps." Lacking these, however, he would most likely have withdrawn angrily into the impotence he exhibits in a most literal form in his encounter with the prostitute.

What the Ohmanns, on the other hand, fail to recognize is that Holden is not looking forward to a better world, but backward to a world that primitivists fancy offered greater freedom to the individual. He seeks not a Marxist society, but a Rousseauesque world. If he is headed anywhere at the time the novel ends, it is not toward a collectivized society, but toward the kind of fragmented "commune" society of small isolated clans with which the hippies experimented. (Much diminished activity of this kind, in fact, still continues in some remote parts of the United States, while a more highly publicized but tiny group still persists in England.)

—Warren French, *J. D. Salinger, Revisited* (Boston: Twayne, 1988), pp. 57–59

[Joyce Rowe is a professor of English at Fordham University and the author of *Equivocal Endings in Classic American Novels* (1988). In this extract, Rowe maintains that Holden's sense of alienation is produced by a kind of psychological self-mutilation.]

Because Holden is never allowed to imagine or experience himself in any significant struggle with others (his bloody fist-fight with Stradlater emphasizes the futility of any gesture that *is* open to him), neither he (nor his creator) can conceive of society as a source of growth, or self-knowledge. In place of a dialectical engagement with others, Holden clings to the kind of inner resistance that keeps exiles and isolates alive. In response to the pressures for "adjustment" which his sanitarium psychiatrists impose, he insists upon the principle that spontaneity and life depend upon "not knowing what you're going to *do* until you do it." If the cost of this shard of freedom is the continuing anxiety which alienation and disaffection bring—of life in a permanent wilderness, so to speak—so be it. Impoverished it may be, but in Holden's sense of "freedom" one can already see foreshadowed the celebrated road imagery of the Beats.

Holden's struggle for a moral purity that the actual corruptions and compromises of American society, or indeed any society, belie is a familiar one to readers of classic American works. But as I have already suggested, for Holden the terms of that struggle are reversed. Unlike nineteenth-century characters, Holden is not an obvious social outsider or outcast to those he lives among. Well-born and well-favored, his appearance, abilities, and manners make him an insider—he belongs. And yet, as the heir of all the ages, blessed with the material splendors of the Promised Land, Holden feels more victim or prisoner than favored son. Like the country at large, he expresses his discomfort, his sense of dis-ease, by squandering his resources—physical, emotional, intellectual—without attempting to utilize them for action and change. But the willful futility of his acts should not blind us to the psychic truth which they reveal. Ultimately Holden is performing a kind of self-mutilation against that part of himself which is hostage to the society that has shaped him. Moreover, while previous American heroes like Hester Prynne and Huck Finn evaded social reality at the cost of denying their human need for others and their likeness to them, Holden's resistance concludes on a wistful note of longing for everybody outside the prison of his sanitarium—an ambivalence that aptly fixes the contemporary terms of his predicament.

Holden's self-division is thus reduced to the only form in which his society can bear to consider it—a psychological problem of acceptance and adjustment; yet Salinger's irony results in a curious double focus. The increasing prestige of American psychoanalysis in the 1950s may be attributed to its tendency (at least in the hands of some practitioners) to sever individual issues and conflicts from their connections to more obdurate realities in the social world. There is familiar comfort in the belief that *all* problems are ultimately individual ones which can, at least potentially, be resolved by force of the individual mind and will. This irony surely lies within the compass of Salinger's story. But its effect is undercut by the polarized perspective that Salinger has imposed on his hero. As we have seen, the stoic isolation through which Holden continues to protect his authenticity is itself an ethic that devalues confrontation or action and so fixes human possibility in the mold of a hopeless hope. Indeed, it becomes a strategy for containment, as much an evasion of social reality as is the psychiatric imperative to adjust.

There is nothing finally in Holden's diffuse sympathies to offend or dismay the reader, nothing to keep him permanently on edge. By the end of the story the reader has seen his familiar social world questioned, shaken, only to be reconstituted as an inevitable fate. Having been drawn to Holden's side we are finally drawn to his mode of perception and defense. To keep the citadel of the self intact by keeping others at a distance is the kind of social agreement that guarantees that the longed-for community which American experience forever promises will surely forever be withheld.

—Joyce Rowe, "Holden Caulfield and American Protest," *New Essays on* The Catcher in the Rye, ed. Jack Salzman (Cambridge: Cambridge University Press, 1991), pp. 90–92

[Sanford Pinsker (b. 1941), a professor of English at Franklin and Marshall College (Lancaster, PA), has written many books on Jewish-American literature, including *The Schlemiel as Metaphor* (1971) and *Jewish-American Fiction 1917–1987* (1992). In this extract, Pinsker studies the conclusion of *The Catcher in the Rye* and speculates on what Holden has learned at the end of his adventures.]

That America has always given rise to a wide variety of dreams is a commonplace idea. What is less apparent perhaps is the ways in which these dreams find themselves realized—usually with heavy doses of irony, and often as nightmares. Call it the peculiarly American shading of the cunning of history. Call it the special consequences, the blessing and curse, of America itself. In any event, the land founded on a great dream has been the beneficiary, and the captive, of dreams ever since. It is a part of what Henry James meant when he called being an American "a complex fate" and what Fitzgerald had in mind as he wrote the final lines of *The Great Gatsby*.

I belabor these matters because, although Holden's "madman weekend" ends in the drenching rains of Central Park with Phoebe "going around and around in her blue coat," the novel itself concludes with Holden in a very different West from the one he fantasized about. As Holden puts it, "I got pretty run-down and had to come out here, and take it easy." The *here* is a rest home not far from Hollywood, where "this one psychoanalyst guy they have here, keeps asking me if I'm going to apply myself when I go back to school next September." Not surprisingly, Holden cannot answer such a question.

Whatever else lies ahead, one thing is clear—Holden, the narrator, no longer clings to the same desperate scenarios that defined him as a participant in his story. His life will be neither as a saintly "catcher in the rye" nor will it include masquerades as a deaf-mute pumping gas in an ill-defined West. For better or worse, when the psychoanalyst rattles on about what his patient will be like next September, Holden listens and makes as honest an effort as he can to respond.

More speculation than this is a mug's game, because characters, even ones as vividly rendered as Holden, do not outlive their last page. When Huck Finn finishes the final paragraph of his adventures, he declares himself "rotten glad" that there's nothing left to tell. Holden also concludes on a note of sorrow, but one that revolves around the idea that if you "tell" about people, even people like Stradlater and Maurice, you end up missing them. After all, they were the ones who put his uncompromising sense of innocence under pressure, and in his farewell to them is also the hint of an ambivalent farewell to a fondly remembered former self.

Besides, without other people there is no story, no human context, and, more important, no humanity. Once again, the Stephen Dedalus of Joyce's *A Portrait of the Artist as a Young Man* may prove an instructive model. Stephen imagines that he can only become the writer he is destined to be when he flies past the nets of family, church, and state. Only then—when he is at last free of everything that exasperates and confines—will he be able to discover his true subject. What Stephen discovers, however, is that there are *no* subjects for fiction other than family, church, and state—whether it be the tale of how one lived among them, how one wriggled free, or how one learned to accommodate them. That lesson comes in *Ulysses,* as Stephen meets the thoroughly human, thoroughly vulnerable Leopold Bloom and learns something about the power of love.

I read Holden's concluding admission that he "misses" everyone as a similar recognition. Granted, love does not come easily to the Holden who spares no pains when it comes to phonies; but there is a greater chance he will temper his righteous indignation than fulfill Mr. Antolini's ominous prophecies about him. Even more important perhaps, Holden's story—despite his regrets about telling it—makes good on Mr. Antolini's notion about the value of keeping a record of one's trouble, and the way that the resulting work might help someone "learn something from you." The fact is that you were drawn to Salinger's novel, and even to this book about that book, is proof that Holden's voice still speaks to those experiencing similar confusions, as well as to those who still harbor a fondness for him tucked somewhere inside their adult facades.

—Sanford Pinsker, The Catcher in the Rye: *Innocence under Pressure* (New York: Twayne, 1993), pp. 95–97

Books by
J. D. Salinger

The Catcher in the Rye. 1951.

Nine Stories. 1953.

Franny and Zooey. 1961.

Raise High the Roof Beam, Carpenters, and Seymour—An Introduction. 1963.

Complete Uncollected Short Stories. c. 1967–74. 2 vols.

Works about
J. D. Salinger and
The Catcher in the Rye

Ahrne, Marianne. "Experience and Attitude in *The Catcher in the Rye* and *Nine Stories*." *Moderna Sprak* 61 (1967): 242–63.

Baskett, S. S. "The Splendid/Squalid World of J. D. Salinger." *Wisconsin Studies in Contemporary Literature* 4 (1966): 48–61.

Belcher, William F., and James W. Lee, ed. *J. D. Salinger and the Critics*. Belmont, CA: Wadsworth, 1962.

Bloom, Harold, ed. *Holden Caulfield*. New York: Chelsea House, 1990.

———, ed. *J. D. Salinger*. New York: Chelsea House, 1987.

Bryan, James. "The Psychological Structure of *The Catcher in the Rye*." *PMLA* 89 (1974): 1065–74.

Burrows, David J. "Allie and Phoebe: Death and Love in Salinger's *The Catcher in the Rye*." In *Private Dealings: Modern American Writers in Search of Integrity,* ed. David J. Burrows, Lewis M. Dabney, Milne Holton, and Grosvenor E. Powell. Rockville, MD: New Perspectives, 1969, pp. 106–14.

Cohen, Hubert I. " 'A Woeful Agony Which Forced Me to Begin My Tale': *The Catcher in the Rye*." *Modern Fiction Studies* 12 (1966–67): 355–66.

Coles, Robert. "A Reconsideration of J. D. Salinger." *New Republic,* 28 April 1973, pp. 30–32.

Costello, Donald P. "The Language of *The Catcher in the Rye*." *American Speech* 34 (1959): 172–81.

Costello, Patrick. "Salinger and 'Honest Iago.' " *Renascence* 16 (1964): 171–74.

Deer, Irving, and John H. Randal III. "J. D. Salinger and the Reality Beyond Words." *Lock Haven Review* No. 6 (1964): 14–29.

French, Warren. "Holden's Fall." *Modern Fiction Studies* 10 (1964–65): 389.

———. *J. D. Salinger.* New York: Twayne, 1963 (rev. ed. 1976).

Furst, Lilian R. "Dostoyevsky's *Notes from the Underground* and Salinger's *The Catcher in the Rye.*" *Canadian Review of Comparative Literature* 5 (1978): 72–85.

Giles, Barbara. "The Lonely War of J. D. Salinger." *Mainstream* 12 (February 1959): 2–13.

Glasser, William. *"The Catcher in the Rye." Michigan Quarterly Review* 15 (1976): 432–57.

Hainsworth, J. D. "Maturity in J. D. Salinger's *The Catcher in the Rye.*" *English Studies* 48 (1967): 426–31.

Hamilton, Ian. *A Search for J. D. Salinger.* New York: Random House, 1988.

Hamilton, Kenneth. *J. D. Salinger: A Critical Essay.* Grand Rapids, MI: Eerdmans, 1967.

Hinckle, Warren, et al. "A Symposium on J. D. Salinger." *Ramparts* 1 (1962): 47–66.

Jacobs, Robert G. "J. D. Salinger's *The Catcher in the Rye:* Holden Caulfield's 'Goddam Autobiography.'" *Iowa English Yearbook* No. 4 (Fall 1959): 9–14.

Kaplan, Charles. "Holden and Huck: The Odysseys of Youth." *College English* 18 (1956–57): 76–80.

Laser, Marvin, and Norman Fruman, ed. *Studies of J. D. Salinger: Reviews, Essays, and Critiques of* The Catcher in the Rye *and Other Fiction.* New York: Odyssey Press, 1963.

Lettis, Richard. "Holden Caulfield: Salinger's 'Ironic Amalgam.'" *American Notes & Queries* 15 (1976): 43–45.

Livingston, James T. "J. D. Salinger: The Artist's Struggle to Stand on Holy Ground." In *Adversity and Grace: Studies in Recent American Literature,* ed. Nathan A. Scott, Jr. Chicago: University of Chicago Press, 1968, pp. 113–32.

Luedtke, Luther S. "J. D. Salinger and Robert Burns: *The Catcher in the Rye.*" *Modern Fiction Studies* 16 (1970–71): 198–201.

Lundquist, James. *J. D. Salinger.* New York: Ungar, 1979.

McNamara, Eugene. "Holden as Novelist." *English Journal* 54 (1965): 166–70.

Marsden, Malcolm M., ed. *If You Really Want to Know: A Catcher Casebook.* Chicago: Scott, Foresman, 1963.

Mitchell, Susan K. " 'To Tell You the Truth. . . .' " *CLA Journal* 36 (1992–93): 145–56.

Nanba, Tatsuro. *The Language of Salinger's* The Catcher in the Rye. Tokyo: Shinozaki, 1984.

O'Hara, J. D. "No Catcher in the Rye." *Modern Fiction Studies* 9 (1963–64): 370–76.

Ohmann, Carol, and Richard Ohmann. "Reviewers, Critics and *The Catcher in the Rye.*" *Critical Inquiry* 3 (Autumn 1976): 15–37.

Olan, Levi A. "The Voice of the Lonesome: Alienation from Huck Finn to Holden Caulfield." *Southwest Review* 48 (1963): 143–50.

Peavy, Charles D. " 'Did You Ever Have a Sister?' Holden, Quentin, and Sexual Innocence." *Florida Quarterly* 1 (1968): 82–95.

Pinsker, Sanford. "*The Catcher in the Rye* and All: Is the Age of Formative Books Over?" *Georgia Review* 40 (1986): 953–67.

Roemer, Danielle M. "The Personal Narrative in Salinger's *The Catcher in the Rye.*" *Western Folklore* 51 (1992): 5–10.

Rosen, Gerald. "A Retrospective Look at *The Catcher in the Rye.*" *American Quarterly* 29 (1977): 547–62.

———. *Zen in the Art of J. D. Salinger.* Berkeley, CA: Creative Arts Book Co., 1977.

Salzberg, Joel, ed. *Critical Essays on Salinger's* The Catcher in the Rye. Boston: G. K. Hall, 1990.

Seng, D. J. "The Fallen Idol: The Immature World of Holden Caulfield." *College English* 23 (1961): 203–9.

Simonson, Harold P., and Philip E. Hager, ed. *Salinger's* Catcher in the Rye: *Clamor vs. Criticism.* Lexington, MA: D. C. Heath, 1963.

Strauch, Carl F. "Kings in the Back Row: Meaning through Structure—A Reading of Salinger's *The Catcher in the Rye.*" *Wisconsin Studies in Contemporary Literature* 2 (1961): 5–30.

Trowbridge, Clinton W. "Hamlet and Holden." *English Journal* 57 (1968): 26–29.

————. "Salinger's Symbolic Use of Character and Detail in *The Catcher in the Rye.*" *Cimarron Review* No. 4 (June 1968): 5–11.

Wakefield, Dan. "Salinger and the Search for Love." *New World Writing No. 14.* New York: New American Library, 1958, pp. 68–85.

Wells, Arvin R. "Huck Finn and Holden Caulfield: The Situation of the Hero." *Ohio University Review* 1 (1960): 31–42.

Wenke, John. *J. D. Salinger: A Study of the Short Fiction.* Boston: Twayne, 1991.

Zapf, Hubert. "Logical Action in *The Catcher in the Rye.*" *College Literature* 12 (1985): 266–71.

Index of
Themes and Ideas